SELF HELP IS NO HELP

How to Stop Fixing Yourself And Start Living Free

I0560870

Marty Hale

STRAIGHT
TRUTH PRESS

Straight Truth Press

ISBN (EPUB): 978-1-968908-01-0
ISBN (Print):   978-1-968908-00-3
First edition, 2025
Printed in the United States of America
Cover and interior design by the author.

For permissions, questions, or spiritual help, contact:
info@straighttruthpress.com

Scripture quotations are taken from the *Yoked Bible Translation*.
Used by permission. All rights reserved.

Table of Contents

Dedication

To the disciples of Jesus who desire to be **YOKED**— not in name only, but in spirit, in discipline, and in truth.

This book is dedicated to the growing community of men and women uniting through **YOKED**— those who are committing their lives to walk in faithful obedience to Christ, to build one another up in **faith,** to strengthen the body in **fitness,** and to steward God's resources through **financial wisdom**.

May your yoke be easy, your burden light, and your joy in the journey complete.

"Take My yoke upon you and learn from Me...
and you will find rest for your souls." —
Matthew 11:29

About the Author

Marty Hale knows what it's like to stand at the top of the mountain—and still feel empty.

He's been named *CEO of the Decade*, led multi-million dollar companies, spoken to thousands, and built high-performance teams across the globe. His expertise in leadership, business, and personal development is recognized by some of the world's most influential organizations.

But none of that could save him.

Behind the titles and achievements is a man who has failed, hurt, been hurt, and come face to face with the truth: **no amount of success can fill the soul.**

Marty is not writing from a pedestal. He's writing as someone who has been broken, humbled, and rescued—not by strategy, not by effort, but by Jesus Christ.

Self Help Is No Help is more than a message—it's a confession, a witness, and a call to come home. Marty's life has been changed not by climbing higher, but by laying everything down at the feet of the only One who saves.

He lives in Lubbock, Texas, and continues to teach, write, and serve—not as a man with all the answers, but as one committed to the only Answer that matters.

Introduction

When Doing More Still Isn't Enough

You didn't pick up this book because everything in your life is working.

Maybe you've read the books, listened to the podcasts, and posted the quotes. You've journaled your way through pain, vision-boarded your future, stacked your habits, optimized your mornings, and rewritten your story so many times that the ink has started to bleed.

And still… the ache remains.

You still lose your temper. Still snap at your kids. Still numb yourself late at night. Still battle guilt, shame, lust, fear, comparison, and the hollow fatigue of pretending you're fine. You've improved in ways that make your coworkers clap and your friends nod—yet deep down, you know something hasn't changed. Not at the core. Not in the places that count. And maybe—if you're honest—you've started to wonder if you're the problem.

That's what self-help does to you. It promises power and progress. But when it doesn't work, it only leaves you with one conclusion: *"I must not be doing it right."*

What If You Were Never Meant to Fix Yourself?

The self-help world says the answers are already inside you. Just dig deeper. Visualize harder. Trust your gut. Manifest your worth. Rewrite your identity. But what if the problem *isn't* a lack of effort?

What if the problem is self?

And what if the only real freedom comes from surrendering the one thing self-help can never touch—your soul?

This book is not about getting stronger. It's not about hustling harder, believing bigger, or finally unlocking your potential.

This book is about the gospel of Jesus Christ—the news that **you cannot save yourself**... and you don't have to.

For the Worn-Out Believer and the High-Performing Skeptic
This book is for the one who used to believe but got burned by religion. It's for the church kid who knew all the right words but still fell apart. It's for the leader who counsels others but privately feels like a fraud. It's for the addict who quit a dozen times and relapsed again last night. It's for the mom who can't stop yelling, the dad who can't stop lying, the teen who can't stop hiding. It's for the ambitious entrepreneur, the overwhelmed teacher, the weary preacher, the numb accountant, the jaded optimist.
It's for you.

What You'll Find in These Pages
You will not find ten easy steps. You will not find a success formula, a daily affirmation guide, or a productivity hack that unlocks happiness.

What you will find is truth—biblical, bold, uncomfortable, freeing truth. You will find the grace of God that meets you not at your best, but at your lowest. You will find Jesus—not as a life coach, not as a spiritual consultant—but as a crucified King who invites you to die with Him… and finally live.

The Journey Ahead

We will start by dismantling the lies. Then we will turn to the truth. And finally, we will walk toward the freedom that no planner, no therapist, no mantra, and no amount of willpower could ever give you.

This isn't about feeling better. This is about being **born again**.

If you've reached the end of yourself— You're in the right place.

Welcome to *Self Help Is No Help*. Let's begin.

1. The Self-Help Myth
Why Fixing Yourself Will Never Set You Free

Mark Turner's office shelf looked like a greatest-hits collection of modern motivation. *Atomic Habits* sat beside *Can't Hurt Me*; Mel Robbins' neon-green *Let Them Theory* leaned against Jordan Peterson's *Twelve Rules for Life*. A leather journal lay open on his desk—clean script, color-coded goals, habit trackers that measured everything from water intake to minutes of mindfulness. He had installed a whiteboard behind the door for quarterly objectives, and his smartwatch pulsed hourly reminders to stretch, breathe, re-center, believe.

Anyone walking in could assume the man behind that desk was winning at life. Mark assumed it himself—until the November morning his wife packed two suitcases, buckled their children into the SUV, and left a note that began, "I'm tired of being another project you optimize."

It wasn't anger that undid him; it was confusion. He had done everything the books prescribed: woke at five, prayed (he thought), kept a gratitude journal, cold-plunged, lifted, intermittent-fasted, built micro-habits, crushed quarterly sales targets, gave his family a bigger house than he'd known growing up. Yet the woman he loved felt invisible beside the relentless machine of his improvement.

For twelve nights he slept on the living-room floor—the bedroom felt accusatory—and reread Mel Robbins under a single lamp until dawn. Rule after rule promised peace once he let people "do their own thing," yet the bed remained empty and the house echoed. On the thirteenth night he closed the book, slid it across the hardwood, and let a silence he had avoided for years fill the room.

That silence became the teacher every self-help manual had missed.

The Engine Behind the Industry
The modern improvement movement did not invent the longing to grow—it merely monetized it. Dale Carnegie told Depression-era Americans they could *win friends*; Napoleon Hill lectured them on *thinking* themselves *rich*. By the time James Clear arrived with 1-percent habit gains, an entire ecosystem of coaches, masterminds, and subscription apps stood ready to sell blueprints for a better you. In 2025 the industry's annual revenue topped thirteen billion dollars, outselling cookbooks and even some categories of fiction. The market's gravitational center is a single conviction: you are both the problem and the solution.

The Gospel of Self-Reliance
That creed resonates because it flatters our instinct for control. A "growth mindset" sounds nobler than raw ambition, yet the underlying promise is identical to the serpent's whisper in Eden—*you will be like God*. Genesis records no pitch about pleasure or rebellion; the offer was elevation through self-reliance. Eat, and you will know. Eat, and you will rise. The moment Eve reached, humanity's default gospel shifted from *God provides* to *I improve*.

Jeremiah watched Israel chase that myth in his day and gave it words that still sting:

> *"This is what the LORD says: Cursed*
> *is the man who trusts in man, who*
> *relies on human strength and turns his*
> *heart away from the LORD. He will be*
> *like a bush in the desert. He will not*
> *see good things when they come. He*
> *will live in parched places in the*
> *wilderness, in a salty land where no*
> *one lives."*
>
> *—Jeremiah 17:5-6*

A Life That Looks Right—Until it Breaks

Mark had mistaken manic growth for rootedness. His journals bulged with metrics, yet his soul dried like that desert shrub. He trusted flesh—refined, quantified, graphically displayed, but still flesh.

The lie persists because it often "works" for a season. James Clear is not wrong that tiny habits accumulate, and Mel Robbins does offer practical tools for boundaries. Early victories taste like transformation. Morning alarms ring, planners fill, weight drops, productivity spikes, dopamine fires.

Then a layoff happens, or a child is diagnosed, or a marriage buckles, and the scaffolding collapses. The system blamed fail-rate; the gospel calls it root-rot.

Law Reveals, But Cannot Heal

Scripture never mocks discipline; it simply refuses to deify it. Paul urged believers to train like athletes, yet he also confessed a deeper impotence:

> *"I don't understand what I do. I don't do what I want to do. Instead, I do the things I hate."*

> *— Romans 7:15*

Self-help teachers quote half that verse as evidence even saints need better habits, but Paul's point was starker: law—any law, secular or sacred—reveals inability, not capacity. The solution is not tighter law; it is interior resurrection.

Jesus sounded almost cruel to ears attuned to hustle when He said, *"Apart from me you can do nothing"* (John 15:5). Nothing? Surely we can at least optimize our calendars. Yet the branch bears fruit only by union, not exertion. Detach it, and frantic waving where a vine once held it will never ripen a single grape.

The Yoke of Grace

Christ's alternative is not passive. *"Take my yoke,"* He says, *"and learn from me"* (Matthew 11:29). A yoke is work, but it is shared work—strength regulated by relationship. The burden becomes light precisely because the stronger partner carries the gravity. Where self-help shouts, "You've got this," Jesus whispers, "I've got you."

The Silence That Saves

Mark began to glimpse that distinction the week his house fell silent. He had excused his spiritual dryness as a side-effect of success: pray on the run, skim a psalm, make it up on Sunday. Now the emptiness confronted him unmedicated by podcasts. On a windy Saturday he walked a local trail he had once timed for cardio but now wandered without earbuds. Bare cottonwoods rattled overhead. A creek he'd never noticed murmured beside the path. He felt, for the first time in years, small—and oddly relieved.

That evening he opened his childhood Bible, untouched since college. Between thin pages lay a photograph of his baptism: a younger Mark rising from water, eyes wide, hair pasted to his forehead, smile raw.

He remembered believing then that grace was not a program but a Person—that surrender could be joy. Somewhere between spreadsheets and step-goals he had traded that Person for principles.

He knelt on the living-room floor and prayed what planners cannot script: "I can't fix this. I can't fix me. If You want the pieces, take them." There were no fireworks, only awareness—rootlets pressing again toward living water.

Recovery was neither instant nor neat. He still woke early, but the 5 a.m. alarm became an invitation rather than a trigger. Sometimes he sat in silence for forty minutes, mind bouncing, heart numb, and considered it prayer because he was present and honest.

He deleted two habit-tracking apps—tools, not masters. He met weekly with his preacher, not for coaching but confession. He wrote letters to his wife without defending himself, acknowledging how his relentless betterment had crowded her humanity.

Months later, they spoke over coffee. She wept at the table because the man across from her no longer radiated intensity;

he radiated need, which paradoxically felt safe. Reconciliation was no guarantee, but its possibility breathed again.

The Death of the Optimizer

What happened to Mark was not an upgrade. It was a small death followed by steady resurrection. The old narrative— *Mark the optimizer*—had to fail so a truer story could surface: *Mark the branch grafted back into the vine.*

Streams and Roots

Modern culture will continue to sell shiny frameworks. Some will help: pay down debt, exercise, plan meals. Yet none can heal the fracture Jeremiah diagnosed. The question is never whether discipline is useful; the question is which stream nourishes its roots.

If the stream is self, every drought will scorch the leaves. If the stream is Christ, even deserts cannot stop the sap. That is why Jesus offers rest before He ever assigns work; rest is the root from which His work grows.

So the myth is not that self-help offers *nothing*; the myth is that it offers **life**. Life is breathed, not built. It cannot be hacked, stacked, or scheduled; it must be received.

Mark's shelf still holds *Atomic Habits*—he finds micro-shifts handy for clutter control. But a new volume sits beside it: a battered Bible, spine re-creased, margins scribbled. On the inside cover he has written Jeremiah 17:7-8 in thick ink:

> *"But blessed is the man who trusts in*
> *the LORD, whose confidence is in*
> *him. He is like a tree planted by water,*

*sending out its roots by stream. It does
not fear when heat comes; its leaves
are always green. It does not worry in a
year of drought and never stops
bearing fruit."*

He no longer tracks how many pages he reads each dawn. He tracks something stranger: days returned to dependence, days his roots drink deep. The metrics are slower, harder to chart—patience under stress, gentleness with his kids, tenderness when memory of failure rises. Yet those fruits last longer than any quarterly goal.

Learning to Breathes Again

One humid spring morning, while pruning the backyard maple, he understood at last why Jesus called pruning love: branches trimmed of self-importance can breathe. He set the shears down, wiped sap from his hands, and thanked God for a yoke that felt at once weighty and weightless—weighty where it crossed his shoulders, weightless where another bore the pull. He had not become the hero of his story. He had met the Hero.

And that, he realized, was the end of the myth and the beginning of freedom.

2. Why You Can't Save Yourself
Because Dead People Can't Rescue Themselves

It was always nights like this that got to him. After the kids were in bed, after the television flickered off, after the house settled into quiet. Jacob sat on the edge of his recliner, staring into a mug of cold coffee that he had reheated twice and never finished.

On the table beside him sat his Bible—closed—and three books about overcoming addiction, none of which he could remember ordering.

He had lasted seventeen days this time. That was a record. He had prayed, fasted, journaled, confessed. He'd met with his accountability partner twice, gone to church both Sundays, even volunteered to help with the men's retreat. And still, just hours earlier, he had caved again—back into the addiction that had haunted him for almost two decades. The rush came, followed by the shame, followed by the lie that always sounded like truth: *you're never going to change.*

Jacob wasn't rebellious. He wasn't lazy. He wasn't unaware. He just couldn't fix it. And that, more than the guilt itself, was what drove him to despair. Because he believed what so many others do: that change was just one layer deeper, one strategy smarter, one commitment stronger.

If he could just try harder, want it more, pray longer, cry louder—maybe that would finally be enough.

It never was.

When Trying Harder Isn't Enough

The most damaging thing about the belief that you can save yourself is that it doesn't feel wrong. It feels responsible. Righteous, even. You carry the weight of your behavior. You own your failures. You put in the work. And if you're religious, you do all of that with a layer of spiritual urgency: praying, reading, serving, repenting.

And when it doesn't work, you assume you failed again. You didn't fast enough. Didn't believe enough. Didn't surrender deeply enough.

But what if the failure isn't yours? What if the system is broken?

What if you're not meant to save yourself?

That's not just a question of theology. It's a question of survival.

Because if your ability to be free rests entirely on your own discipline, your own resolve, your own strength—then all you have is the strength of your flesh. And the flesh, no matter how religious or refined, is still at war with the Spirit.

A Cry for Rescue—Not a Plan

Paul understood that tension better than anyone. He wasn't soft on sin. He didn't offer excuses. He called believers to die to self, to resist the flesh, to run the race. But Paul also confessed what many modern believers are too ashamed to say: *I want to do what's right—and I still don't.*

> *"I don't understand what I do. I don't*
> *do what I want to do. Instead, I do the*
> *things I hate."*
>
> —*Romans 7:15*

That's not spiritual immaturity. That's the cry of a man who knows the law but cannot escape his own nature. And Paul doesn't resolve the tension by saying, *I just need to try harder next time.*

He cries out, *"Who will rescue me from this dying body?"*

Not *what will rescue me.* Not a strategy. Not a method. Not a plan. A *Person.*

> *"Thanks be to God—through Jesus*
> *Christ our Lord!"*
>
> —*Romans 7:25*

Paul doesn't find freedom in a more determined self.

He finds it in surrender to a better Savior.

How We Turn Faith Into Self-Help

We are a people addicted to control. Not just in our behaviors, but in our redemption. We want a faith that lets us remain in charge. We want to manage our healing like a checklist, reduce repentance to behavior change, and treat grace as a divine push at the start line—but run the rest of the race in our own strength.

Even our spiritual disciplines can become self-reliance in disguise. We read, pray, tithe, and serve not to abide in Christ but to try and prove that we're getting better. That we're worthy. That we're fixing it.

We don't come to the cross. We work around it.

And when we stumble—again—we spiral in shame. Or worse, we redouble our effort, believing that what failed before will succeed if we can just want it more. That's not repentance. That's legalism. And it is every bit as exhausting as it is powerless.

Jesus Didn't Come to Make You Better

Jesus didn't come to help you fix yourself. He came to raise you from the dead.

The gospel isn't about giving you a second chance. It's about giving you a new heart.

> *"I will give you a new heart and put a new spirit in you. I will take away your heart of stone and give you a heart of flesh. I will put my Spirit in you and move you to follow my commands and be careful to do what i say."*
>
> *—Ezekiel 36:26–27*

That's not poetry. That's the actual mechanism of salvation.

You don't climb your way into righteousness. You are made new—by God's initiative, not your effort. The Spirit takes up residence, not because you proved yourself worthy, but because you admitted you couldn't.

The clearest picture of this is the conversation between Jesus and Nicodemus. A Pharisee. A religious elite. A man who had tried everything the law prescribed. And Jesus doesn't congratulate him on his effort.

He says, *"You must be born again."* (John 3:7)

Not improved. Not cleaned up. Not rebooted.

Born again. A new creation, with a new nature, and a new Source of life.

That's the gospel.

And it leaves no room for saving yourself.

The Gospel Leaves No Room for Self-Salvation
But we resist this, even as believers. Something in us clings to the illusion of control. We want grace, but we want to feel like we've earned it. We want to surrender, but only on our own terms. We want transformation, but without the humiliation of admitting that we are absolutely powerless to produce it.

We would rather fail on our own than be rescued in weakness.

But God is not interested in co-authoring your salvation story. He's not your coach. He's not your consultant. He's not waiting for your performance to meet Him halfway.

He is your Redeemer. And the only part you bring to your redemption is the sin that made it necessary.

That's the message that breaks the back of pride and gives life to the soul.

> *"For it is God who is working in you both to will and to work for his good purpose."*
>
> —*Philippians 2:13*

Did you catch that? Even your *desire* to do good comes from Him.

You don't have to manufacture your own willpower.

You yield.

You trust.

You surrender.

Learning to Abide Instead of Strive

For Jacob, this realization came slowly, painfully. After that night of failure, he called his mentor and finally told the truth—not the half-truths he had shared before, not the versions of struggle that still made him sound devout, but the raw, unfiltered confession: "I can't beat this. I've tried everything."

His mentor didn't give him another book. He didn't assign a new plan. He simply said, "You're ready now."

"Ready for what?"

"To stop fighting alone. To stop trying to be your own Savior."

They met every week—not for strategy, but for prayer. Not for discipline, but for dependency. They opened the Word together. Not looking for tips, but for **truth**. They fasted—not to earn God's favor, but to remind Jacob of his hunger. His need. His weakness.

Over time, something shifted.

Not in his effort—but in his posture.

He stopped striving to escape failure.

He started learning how to abide.

The Freedom of Resting in Christ
The freedom Jacob found didn't come from more resistance.

It came from resting in the One who had already overcome.

He started to believe, really believe, that Jesus didn't come to give him one more chance to get it right.

He came to be his righteousness.

And that truth—that Christ was not just the goal, but the means—changed everything.
Jacob didn't stop struggling overnight.

But the shame lost its power.

The spiral lost its momentum.

Because he no longer measured his worth by his performance. He measured it by the finished work of the cross.

That's the shift every Christian must make if we want to walk in the freedom Jesus actually purchased.

Not, *"I must do better because I've failed."*

But, *"Christ has already done what I could never do—so I trust Him."*

Dying to Self—And Rising Again
This isn't passivity. This isn't resignation. This is **biblical surrender**.

It's what Paul meant when he said:

> *"I have been crucified with Christ, and
> I no longer live, but Christ lives in me.
> The life I now live in the flesh, I live by
> faith in the Son of God, who loved me
> and gave himself for me."*
>
> *—Galatians 2:20*

You don't white-knuckle your way to freedom.

You die.
And you rise again—not by your strength, but by His Spirit.

> *"And if the Spirit of him who raised
> Jesus from the dead lives in you, then
> he who raised Christ from the dead will*

*also give life to your mortal bodies
through His Spirit who lives in you."*

—*Romans 8:11*

This is the life we're invited to.

Not constant self-correction, but **Spirit-empowered transformation**.

Not more willpower, but deeper worship.

Not proving ourselves, but proclaiming His sufficiency.

***

So What...

If you're still trying to fix yourself, hear this:

You can't. And you don't have to.

That's not failure. That's freedom.

God never asked you to save yourself. He asked you to trust Him.

So this week, do one thing:

Stop pretending you're stronger than you are.

Admit it.

Say it aloud.

Pray what Jacob prayed:

> *"I've tried everything.*
> *I can't fix this.*
> *I need You."*

Then sit.

Let the silence speak.

Let the striving stop.

Let the gospel take over.

Because the best news in the world isn't that you get another chance.

It's that Jesus came to do what you never could.

He didn't come to help you climb.

He came to carry you home.

3. The Gospel vs. the Grind
How the Gospel Frees You from Performance-Based Worth

He was the kind of Christian people pointed to when they wanted to feel inspired. Early to church. First to volunteer. The guy who stayed late stacking chairs while others scrolled their phones in the parking lot. His name was Adam, and he wasn't just dependable—he was consistent. He tithed, he served, he read Scripture with his kids at breakfast. He was everything he thought a man of God should be.

But what nobody knew—what not even his wife could see most days—was how tired he was.

Not physically, though that too. Not emotionally, though the tension had started to show around the edges of his marriage. No, Adam was spiritually tired. Exhausted in the deepest, most hidden way a soul can be exhausted.

Because he was doing everything right.

And none of it felt like life.

When Doing Everything Right Still Feels Empty
There's a kind of Christianity that looks beautiful on the surface. It's structured. It's obedient. It's morally upright. It's sacrificial. And it's dead.

Not because the actions are wrong, but because the motive has become corrupted. The grind has replaced the gospel. The doing has replaced the receiving. And what started as gratitude becomes a treadmill of performance.

This isn't just a modern problem. It's an ancient one.

The Older Brother Syndrome

Jesus told a story about two sons.

One rebelled and ran. The other stayed and worked.

We often focus on the younger son—the prodigal, the wanderer, the repentant fool who returns home.

But it's the older brother that Jesus leaves hanging at the end of the parable.

The older brother had stayed. He had served. He had honored. He had done what was right.

But when grace was extended to the undeserving, he was furious.

> *"Look, I've been slaving away for you all these years," he said. "I never disobeyed. I never strayed. I never stopped grinding. And what do I get for it? Not even a goat to celebrate with my friends."*
> *(Luke 15:29–30, paraphrased)*

He didn't understand the Father's heart.

Because deep down, **he didn't feel like a son. He felt like a servant.**

He hadn't been living in grace.

He'd been grinding for approval he already had.

Serving Without Resting
That's where Adam found himself. Not in rebellion. Not in sin. But in performance.

In the subtle, soul-wearing belief that God was more pleased with him when he was useful.

He would never say it out loud, but he believed grace had a limit. That the blood of Jesus covered the past, but sanctification was his job now. That God expected a return on investment—and Adam intended to deliver it.

So he served.
He prayed.
He read.
He led.
He smiled.
He ground it out.
And inside, he grew emptier by the day.

The Panic Beneath the Performance
At first, he blamed external things. Maybe he wasn't resting enough. Maybe he needed to rework his devotional schedule. Maybe he wasn't leading his family with enough intentionality. He redoubled his efforts. Got up earlier. Memorized more Scripture. Listened to more sermons. Downloaded a new Bible app that tracked reading and offered badges for streaks.

But the more he did, the less he felt.

And then came the panic: *What's wrong with me?*

That's what performance religion always produces—panic or pride. Panic when you fall short. Pride when you think you're doing better than others.

Both are rooted in a gospel that has been replaced by a grind.

When Effort Replaces the Spirit
Paul confronted this exact dynamic in the churches of Galatia.

They had received the Spirit. They had been saved by grace. But something changed.

They began to believe that spiritual maturity came through human effort.

So Paul writes:

> *"I only want to learn this from you:*
> *Did you receive the Spirit by works of*
> *the law or by believing what you*
> *heard? Are you so foolish? After*
> *beginning by the Spirit, are you now*
> *being finishing in the flesh?"*

—*Galatians 3:2–3*

It's not a rhetorical question. It's a rebuke.

They had started with surrender—and moved to self-effort. They had forgotten the gospel and embraced the grind.

Not out of rebellion, but out of insecurity.

And Paul calls them back.

The Night the Grind Broke

Adam eventually cracked.

It wasn't dramatic. No scandal. No collapse. Just a quiet night at home, sitting on the edge of his bed, staring at the ceiling and whispering, "I don't feel You anymore."

He hadn't felt God's presence in months. Maybe years.

Not because God was gone.

But because Adam had buried grace beneath performance.

That night, he pulled out his Bible—not out of habit, but hunger. He turned to Matthew 11, where he had read a hundred times before, and for the first time in his life, it felt like an invitation rather than a duty.

> *"Come to me, all you who are weary*
> *and burdened, and I will give you rest.*
> *Take My yoke upon you and learn*
> *from me, because I am gentle and*
> *humble in heart, and you will find rest*
> *for your souls. For My yoke is easy and*
> *my burden is light."*
>
> *—Matthew 11:28–30*

He read it aloud.

Then again.

And for the first time in a long time, he cried.

Not because he had failed.

But because he had never needed to try so hard in the first place.

The Real Jesus Doesn't Demand Your Résumé

Jesus is not impressed by your spiritual résumé.

He's not waiting for you to earn your place at His table.

He is the one who girded Himself with a towel and washed the feet of men who would all abandon Him.

He is the one who welcomes tax collectors and prostitutes, not after they clean themselves up, but when they admit they can't.

He is the one who looks at exhausted believers and says: *Put down your grind. Pick up My grace.*

That doesn't mean stop obeying. It means stop obeying as a way to prove you're worthy.

Obedience Is Not Obligation

There's a difference between obedience and obligation.

Obedience is the response of a son who knows he is loved.

Obligation is the striving of a servant who fears he will never measure up.

The gospel produces the first.

Religion produces the second.

Grace Covers Your Effort, Too
Jesus didn't die so you could grind harder.

He died so you could live free.

> *"So if the Son sets you free,*
> *you really will be free."*
>
> *—John 8:36*

Free from shame.
Free from striving.
Free from the fear that you're never enough.

Because He is enough.

And that's the scandal of grace.

It doesn't just cover your sin.

It covers your effort.

It saves you not only from unrighteousness, but from self-righteousness.

What Changed for Adam
For Adam, that realization changed everything.

Slowly, his spiritual life began to feel like life again.

He didn't stop serving. He didn't abandon the habits.

But he stopped grinding.

He started waking up not to perform, but to commune.

He prayed less like a soldier reporting for duty and more like a son sitting at the Father's table.

And when he failed—when he missed a day, or forgot a verse, or skipped a fast—he didn't spiral into shame.

He remembered that his righteousness was not in his record, but in Christ's.

Gospel vs. Grind
That's the difference between the gospel and the grind.

The grind says, *Try harder.*
The gospel says, *Trust deeper.*
The grind says, *You've got this.*
The gospel says, *He already did.*
The grind says, *Make it happen.*
The gospel says, *It is finished.*

The Freedom to Abide
You can obey with joy when you stop obeying for approval.

You can pursue holiness when you know it doesn't earn you love—it flows from it.

You can be free from the tyranny of doing enough.

Because in Jesus, you are already enough.

***

So what does that look like?

It looks like Sabbath—not just in your schedule, but in your soul.
It looks like prayer without performance.
Scripture without scoring.
Service without scoreboard.
It looks like breathing.
Trusting.
Receiving.
Resting.
Abiding.

Fruit Comes from Connection, Not Pressure

> *"Remain in Me, and I will remain in you.*
> *Just as a branch cannot bear fruit by itself*
> *unless it remains in the vine, neither can*
> *you unless you remain in me."*

> *—John 15:4*

The fruit comes not from the pressure, but from the connection.

Not from the grind, but from the gospel.

The gospel that says: you don't have to run yourself into the ground to be found.

You don't have to earn what was already paid for.
You don't have to achieve what was freely given.
You are not what you accomplish.

You are who He rescued.
And that rescue is finished.
Complete.
Enough.

So What...
Where are you still grinding?

Where have you substituted performance for intimacy?

Where are you living like a servant when God has already called you His child?

This week, stop measuring.
Stop counting.
Stop trying to earn what was never for sale.

Read Scripture not to win a badge, but to hear your Father's voice.

Pray not to impress Him, but to be with Him.

Rest—not because you've done enough, but because He has.

Let the gospel do what the grind never could.

Let grace carry what your effort could never hold.

Come to Him.
You'll find rest.
And in that rest, you'll find life.

4. When Trying Harder Makes Things Worse
What God Does That Your Willpower Never Can

Casey had done everything the book said.

She had her morning routine dialed in: wake at 5:30, gratitude journal, read a chapter of Proverbs, thirty minutes of cardio, protein shake, and then a daily affirmations app that popped up with phrases like, *"You are strong. You are capable. You are worthy."*

Her life looked like a self-help success story.

She had color-coded lists. She had a weekly "reset" day. She used four different productivity apps. She avoided sugar, social media, and negativity. She prayed each morning and finished each day with a five-minute reflection.

And she was falling apart.

Not in a way you'd notice from the outside. Her Instagram was still curated. Her small group still admired her. Her Bible still had fresh underlines in four different colors.

But her heart was brittle. Her joy was gone. Her relationship with God felt cold and transactional. The more she did, the more she felt like she was losing something essential—like a woman in a sinking boat who keeps bailing water, unaware that the real problem is a hole she can't see.

The truth was simple and devastating: the harder she tried, the worse things got.

And she had no idea why.

The Effort Illusion
We've been sold a lie that effort is always the answer.

That failure is always the result of not trying hard enough.

That if you're still struggling, still anxious, still falling short, the solution is to double down. To dig deeper. To recommit.

Try harder.
Pray more.
Work smarter.
Eliminate distractions.
Cut off negativity.

It's the same lie, dressed in different robes—whether it's the CEO on YouTube or the preacher at the women's retreat. If you're not better yet, you haven't tried hard enough.

But Scripture tells a different story.

There are times when trying harder not only fails—it makes things worse.

Because it draws you further away from the only real source of change: surrender.

The Dead-End of the Flesh
Paul said it plainly in Romans 7. This wasn't a confession of willpower failure. It was a declaration of the spiritual dead-end of the flesh.

"I know nothing good lives in me—
that is, in my flesh. I want to do what is
right, but I can't make it happen. I
don't do the good I want to do. Instead,
I do the evil I don't want to do."

—*Romans 7:18–19*

This wasn't the language of rebellion.

It was the language of defeat.

And it's a defeat that effort can't overcome—because the issue isn't laziness or lack of commitment.

It's the nature of the flesh.

White-Knuckle Religion Fails Every Time

Trying harder, in the flesh, doesn't lead to holiness.

It leads to frustration, shame, exhaustion, and often self-deception.

It leads you into a cycle of short-term zeal followed by long-term collapse.

You white-knuckle your way through a week of good habits.

You post a few verses. You fast a few meals. You swear this time is different.

And when the inevitable failure comes, it hits harder than before—because you were trying so hard.

Now not only have you failed, but you've wasted your best effort.

And the next time, it's harder to believe.

A Cry on the Shoulder of the Road
Casey's breaking point came on a Thursday morning.

She was driving to work, listening to a sermon on spiritual discipline, and crying—not because she was convicted, but because she felt like she was drowning in a gospel that offered no air.

She pulled over on the side of the highway and screamed into the steering wheel: **"What more do You want from me?"**

She wasn't angry at God as much as she was defeated by her inability to find Him in all her effort.

She was trying to climb her way into His presence.

Trying to impress Him with consistency.

Trying to manage grace like a resource that could run out.

And in doing so, she had cut herself off from the very thing she needed most.

Self-Made Religion Has No Power
Paul wrote to the Colossians about this exact problem. He warned them against adding human effort to what Christ had already finished.

> *"If you died with Christ to the*
> *elemental forces of the world, why do*
> *you submit to regulations as though you*
> *were still living in the world? Don't*
> *handle, don't taste, don't touch? All*
> *these things refer to the things that*
> *perish with use and are based on human*
> *commands and teaching. Although*
> *these have an appearance of wisdom in*
> *promoting self-made religion, false*
> *humility, and severe treatment of the*
> *body, they are not of any value in*
> *restraining fleshly indulgence."*

> *—Colossians 2:20–23*

Did you catch that?

Self-made religion—even disciplined, rigorous, sacrificial religion—has *no power* to transform the heart.

It can polish the outside.

But it cannot save the inside.

And worse—it can blind you into thinking you're making progress when you're really just wearing yourself out.

Grace Works From—Not For—Salvation
The tragedy of the try-harder gospel is that it sounds biblical.

After all, the Bible calls us to work out our salvation, to run the race, to put sin to death, to be holy.

But every single one of those commands is rooted in **grace**, not grit.

You're not working *for* salvation. You're working *from* it.

You're not running to prove your worth. You're running because you've been set free.

You're not killing sin alone. You're partnering with the Spirit who already lives in you.

> *"For if you live according to the flesh, you will die. But if by the Spirit you put to death the deeds of the body, you will live."*
>
> —*Romans 8:13*

"By the Spirit."

Not by effort alone.

"When Did You Stop Letting God Love You?"

When Casey finally broke, it wasn't because her habits failed. It was because her heart was never meant to carry the weight of self-redemption.

She made an appointment with a counselor—something she had been avoiding because she feared it would be admitting defeat.

But what she found in that first session wasn't shame.

It was clarity.

The counselor listened to her spiritual to-do list. Then asked a simple question:

"When did you stop letting God love you?"

Casey blinked.

She had never thought of it that way.

She had been so busy trying to *show* God her love that she had forgotten what it meant to *receive* His.

How Trying Harder Becomes Spiritual Self-Sabotage

This is where trying harder becomes dangerous.

Because it's not just exhausting.

It's deceptive.

It convinces you that you're doing better spiritually while you're actually drifting further from grace.

It turns sanctification into self-discipline.

It turns prayer into performance.

It turns quiet time into a quota.

And eventually, it turns faith into a formula that no longer includes the cross.

Missing Jesus in All the Doing

Jesus said something shocking to the Pharisees in John 5.

These were men who knew Scripture. Men who searched the Word daily. Men who lived cleaner lives than most modern believers.

But Jesus says:

> *"You search the Scriptures because*
> *you think that in them you have eternal*
> *life. And it is they that testify about*
> *me, yet you refuse to come to me that*
> *you may have life."*

> —*John 5:39–40*

They were doing the right things.

But they missed the Person those things pointed to.

You can master every Bible study, nail every journal prompt, hit every reading plan—and still miss Jesus.

Trying harder doesn't guarantee transformation.
Coming to Him does.

From Effort to Intimacy
So what does it look like to stop trying harder?

Not to become passive. Not to be careless. But to shift from effort to intimacy.

It looks like sitting before God without a checklist.

It looks like confessing weakness instead of hiding behind disciplines.

It looks like laying down the idol of progress and picking up the posture of a child.

It looks like admitting: *"I can't fix this. I can't transform myself. I can't manufacture freedom."*

It looks like surrender.

The Cost—and Beauty—of Surrender
And surrender, while simple, is not easy.

Because it kills your pride.

It means admitting you're not in control.

It means trusting that God will finish what He started, even if it doesn't follow your timeline or method.

It means resting before the victory comes.

Waiting before the answer shows up.

Believing when there's no measurable improvement.

That kind of faith doesn't produce Instagram content.

But it produces life.

Abide, Don't Perform
Casey didn't abandon her structure.

But she stopped using it to measure her worth.

She still read Scripture. But now it was for communion, not completion.

She still journaled. But now it included messier prayers.

She still served. But now it flowed from joy, not obligation.

And for the first time in a long time, she felt like she was walking *with* God—not performing *for* Him.

She stopped grinding and started abiding.

She stopped managing grace and started receiving it.

She stopped pushing and started listening.

And slowly, the soul that had grown dry began to feel like a garden again.

Let Him Finish What He Started

You were never meant to be your own Savior.

Not in your justification.

Not in your sanctification.

Not in your healing.

Not in your growth.

Every inch of your journey with Jesus is fueled by His power, not your discipline.

"I am sure of this: that he who began a
good work in you will carry it on to
completion until the day of Christ Jesus."

—*Philippians 1:6*

Let Him.

Let Him carry what you can't.

Let Him speak where your strategies have failed.

Let Him restore what your hustle has drained.

So What...
If you've been trying harder and getting worse—take it as mercy, not failure.
God is not asking for your effort.

He's asking for your surrender.

He's not grading your performance.

He's inviting you to trust.

This week, do something radical.

Stop pushing.

Start praying.

Stop fixing.

Start listening.

Don't add another rule.

Ask for more of His presence.

Not because you've earned it.

But because He promised it.

And He never breaks a promise.

5. From Self-Reliance to Surrender
How God Meets You at the End of Yourself

By every measurable standard, Logan was winning.

He had built a successful company from the ground up. His name was respected. His marriage had weathered storms and grown stronger. He had three kids who all knew Jesus and still liked spending time with him. He tithed faithfully, mentored young men, and volunteered every other weekend with a ministry that served single moms.

He was the picture of responsible manhood. Self-made, self-managed, and spiritually minded.

But beneath the surface, Logan's confidence in God had slowly been replaced by confidence in himself.

Not in an arrogant, chest-thumping way. He would never say it out loud. He still prayed, still studied Scripture, still asked for the Spirit's help. But over time, surrender had become a slogan—not a posture. When decisions came, he relied on instinct. When obstacles hit, he made a plan. When stress rose, he outworked it.

He trusted God, yes.

But he trusted himself more.

The Slow Unraveling of Strength
Self-reliance doesn't always come as rebellion. Most often, it comes dressed as maturity. We grow. We get stronger. We

make progress. And somewhere along the way, we stop depending on God the way we used to.

We still talk about trust. Still preach surrender. But when life presses in, we default to our old training: fix it, push through, carry it.

That's what Logan did. Until the day his strength failed him.

It wasn't a major collapse. No public scandal. Just a slowly unraveling series of decisions that exposed his blind spots. One deal went bad. Then another. Then another. He took shortcuts. He stopped listening to wise counsel. His pride became obvious to everyone but himself. His marriage, once strong, grew silent and cold. His health deteriorated. His prayer life dried up.

By the time he hit bottom, he realized what he had truly lost. Not the money. Not the opportunities. But the intimacy he once had with God—back when he still needed Him.

Why Self-Sufficiency Starves the Soul

This is the great irony of self-reliance: it feels like strength, but it leads to spiritual starvation.

The more you carry, the more you convince yourself that you're the one who must carry it.

And the longer you live in that pattern, the harder it becomes to lay it down.

That's why Scripture never celebrates self-sufficiency. In fact, it condemns it. Over and over again, God calls people not to build themselves up, but to be broken before Him. Not to strengthen their grip, but to open their hands.

> *"Trust in the Lord with all your heart,*
> *and do not lean on your own*
> *understanding. In all your ways*
> *acknowledge him, and he will make*
> *your paths straight."*
>
> —*Proverbs 3:5–6*

It's not just advice. It's a warning.

Don't lean on yourself. You will fall.

Moses: Zeal Without Dependence

Moses had to learn this the hard way. Raised with power, trained in leadership, fluent in two cultures—he was, in many ways, the ideal deliverer for Israel. He saw the injustice. He hated the oppression. He had the heart to do something about it.

So he acted.

He killed an Egyptian slave driver with his bare hands and buried the body in the sand.

But it wasn't time.

It wasn't God's plan.

And it wasn't surrender.
It was Moses, full of conviction and empty of dependence, taking matters into his own hands.

What followed wasn't a celebration. It was exile. Forty years in the wilderness, tending sheep, forgotten by men, and humbled by God. Until the day a bush caught fire and a voice called out—and the man who once thought he could do it all said, "Please, Lord, send someone else."

Only then was he ready.

Because only then was he weak enough to depend.

Power Perfected in Weakness
Paul said it like this:

> *"But he said to me, 'My grace is sufficient for you. for my power is made perfect in weakness.' Therefore I will boast all the more gladly of my weaknesses, so that the power of Christ may rest upon me."*

> *—2 Corinthians 12:9*

This wasn't poetic humility. It was survival.

Paul had suffered more than most believers can imagine. He had seen the edge of death, tasted betrayal, endured sickness, persecution, anxiety, and physical torment. But his greatest strength was not his resilience—it was his dependence.

Because dependence is the soil of power in the kingdom of God.

Tears in the Counselor's Office
Logan found this out in a counselor's office. He hadn't wanted to go. Men like him fixed their own problems. They

read books. They made calls. They listened to podcasts. But a friend had urged him—more like begged him—to talk to someone who could help.

He was three minutes in when the tears came.

Not because the counselor said anything profound, but because Logan finally admitted what he had worked so hard to hide.

He wasn't enough.

He wasn't strong enough to carry it all.

He wasn't wise enough to navigate the weight of a life that was spinning out of control.

He had built a good life. But he had built it on himself.

And now, it was crumbling.

Surrender is a Daily Posture, Not a One-Time Event
Surrender isn't a one-time decision. It's a daily choice to place your trust in God's ability rather than your own. It's waking up and admitting: *I don't have what it takes today.* It's refusing to depend on yesterday's insight or last week's success. It's falling to your knees before the pressure builds and saying: *Father, if You don't go with me, I won't go.*

Jesus Himself modeled this.

The Son of God—the One through whom all things were made—lived in constant dependence on the Father.

> *"Jesus answered them, Truly, truly, I tell you, the Son is not able to do anything by himself, but only what he sees the Father doing. For whatever the Father does, the Son also does in the same way."*

> —John 5:19

If that was true for Jesus, how much more is it true for us?

The Freedom of Admitting Need

There's a strange freedom that comes when you finally stop pretending to be strong.

You stop over-explaining your failures.
You stop over-compensating for your insecurities.
You stop over-working to stay ahead of your fears.

You begin to let God be God again.

And you realize He never asked you to be Him.

You were never meant to bear the weight of omniscience.

Never meant to be all-sufficient, always composed, always decisive, always stable.

You were made to need.

You were created to lean.

And the more you resist that truth, the more brittle your soul becomes.

Rebuilding on Dependence, Not Drive

Logan didn't turn everything around overnight. There were debts to pay, apologies to make, consequences to walk through. But for the first time in years, his prayer life felt real again. His heart softened. His marriage thawed. And he stopped walking into each day trying to conquer it.

He started meeting it with humility.

With open hands.

With questions instead of declarations.

He gave up trying to manage the outcomes and focused instead on walking closely with God, whatever came.

He began to rebuild his life—not on drive, but on dependence.

When God Changes Your Source

We often ask God to change our circumstances when what He really wants is to change our source.

We want relief.
He wants surrender.

Because until we let go of our illusion of control, we cannot receive the fullness of His power.

The paradox of the gospel is that the path to strength begins with weakness.

The door to freedom opens through brokenness.

The joy of the Lord is not for those who prove themselves but for those who collapse into grace.

Be Still—and Know

> *"Be still, and know that I am God. I will be exalted among the nations, I will be exalted in the earth."*
>
> —*Psalm 46:10*

Be still.
Not produce.
Not grind.
Not manage.
Be still—and know.

That kind of stillness is uncomfortable. It feels unproductive. It feels passive. But it's actually the most powerful place you can be.

It's the place where idols die and trust is born.

It's the place where you stop needing a backup plan and start letting the Spirit lead.

It's the place where control gives way to communion.

It's where you learn that surrender isn't the end of effort.

It's the beginning of effectiveness.

Because now, you're no longer pushing your own agenda.

You're moving in rhythm with a power far greater than yours.

And He knows what you don't.

Let It Fall: The Invitation to Collapse Into Grace

Maybe you've been white-knuckling your way through a season. Maybe your faith is real, but your anxiety is louder. Maybe you believe in God's love but live like it depends on your consistency. Maybe you're the one others lean on, but deep down you're drowning under the weight of holding it all together.

Let it fall.
Let it all fall.

Not irresponsibly. Not recklessly. But honestly.

Let your strength fail.
Let your composure crack.

Let your pride shatter.

Not because you've given up—but because you're finally ready to trust the One who never does.

Unless the Lord Builds the House

> *"Unless the Lord builds the house,*
> *those who build it labor in vain. Unless*
> *the Lord guards the city, the*
> *watchman stay awake in vain."*

—*Psalm 127:1*

You can build.
You can watch.

But if it's not God doing the work, it won't last.

And worse—it will wear you out.

The Beautiful Risk of Surrender
Surrender is scary. It means giving up control. It means stepping into unknown territory. It means acknowledging that your best thinking got you here—and it's not enough.

But it's also beautiful.

Because the God who invites your surrender is the same One who gave up His own Son for your redemption.
He's not waiting to punish you.

He's waiting to carry you.

He's not disappointed in your collapse.

He's been drawing you toward it—so He can rebuild something better.

Something not built on you.

But on Him.

So What...

Where in your life are you still relying on yourself?

Where are you pretending to be strong when you're actually drowning?

Where are you trusting your own understanding instead of God's wisdom?

Where are you pushing when He's calling you to be still?

This week, take a real inventory.

Not of your goals, but of your source.

Ask the hard questions.

And when you find the places where you've been standing on your own strength—

Fall down.

Not to be defeated.

But to be held.

He's waiting.

6. Grace, Not Grit
Why You Can't Earn What God Only Gives

Elena had always been a hard worker.

She took pride in it. She never missed deadlines. Never made excuses. If something needed to get done, she'd do it. Period. She grew up in a family that believed in the gospel but also preached a quiet gospel of hustle. Work hard. Be strong. Don't quit.

So when she became a Christian in college, the transition felt natural. She brought that same mentality to her faith. She read her Bible daily. She volunteered, memorized Scripture, went on mission trips, gave generously, served in every ministry she could find.

At first, it seemed like she was thriving.

But slowly, something changed.

The joy started to fade. Her time with God felt more like performance than relationship. The harder she pushed, the more exhausted she became. She still smiled, still served, still looked the part — but inside, she was drying up.

When her friend asked her how she was really doing, Elena broke down. "I'm tired of trying to be good enough," she whispered. "I know I'm saved by grace. I just don't know how to live by it."

When Grit Replaces Grace

That's the tension so many believers live in. We say we believe in grace, but we try to live by grit.

We know we didn't earn salvation — but then we spend the rest of our Christian lives trying to earn the sense that we're still okay.

It's like grace gets you in the door, but grit is what keeps you in the house.

And somewhere along the way, Christianity becomes less about being loved and more about being useful.

Less about Christ in you, more about you proving yourself to Christ.

And the results are devastating — burnout, anxiety, pride, shame, and in many cases, complete spiritual collapse.

Not because people stopped loving Jesus.

But because they never learned how to stop performing.

The Galatian Warning

Paul saw this happening to the Galatians, and he didn't mince words:

> *"You foolish Galatians! Who has cast a spell on you, before whose eyes Jesus Christ was publicly portrayed as crucified? I only want to learn this from you: Did you receive the Spirit by the works of the law or by believing*

what you heard? Are you so foolish?
After beginning by the Spirit, are you
now finishing in the flesh?"

—Galatians 3:1-3

They had begun with grace — radical, undeserved, Spirit-fueled grace.

And now they were reverting to grit.

Trying to finish what God had started.

Trying to grow themselves.

Trying to earn what had been given freely.

Trying to become holy through human effort.

Paul was appalled. Not because they were immoral. But because they were missing the point of the gospel entirely.

Grace Is the Engine, Not the Entry
Grace is not a starting point. It's the whole path.

It doesn't just save you — it sustains you.

It doesn't just forgive your sin — it reshapes your desires.

It doesn't just wipe the slate clean — it writes a new story on your soul.

That's why Paul said,

> *"By the grace of God I am what I am,*
> *and His grace toward me was not*
> *wasted. Instead, I worked harder than*
> *all of them—yet not I, but the grace of*
> *God that was with me."*

—*1 Corinthians 15:10*

Paul wasn't passive. He didn't sit back and float through life. He worked — hard.

But the engine wasn't grit. It was grace.

Grit says, "I have to do this."
Grace says, "Christ is doing this in me."

Grit says, "Don't mess up."
Grace says, "Even when you do, I'm not leaving."

Grit demands results.
Grace invites relationship.

Grit compares, competes, and constantly questions whether it's enough.
Grace rests in the finished work of the cross.

Why Merit Thinking Runs Deep
Why is this so hard to believe?

Because everything in the world around us runs on merit.

You want a raise? Perform.

You want respect? Earn it.

You want followers? Impress.

We are surrounded by systems that reward effort and punish failure.

So we bring that same mentality into the kingdom of God.

We make discipleship into a productivity app.

We measure spirituality by consistency.

We evaluate worth based on fruitfulness.

We assume God feels about us the way we feel about ourselves on our worst days.

And slowly, almost imperceptibly, we begin living as if grace was just a theological idea — not the living, breathing, animating force of Christian life.

But grace isn't soft.

It isn't passive.

It doesn't just tolerate you — it transforms you.

Not by shaming you into better behavior.

Not by exhausting you with rules.

But by meeting you in your lowest place and speaking a better word.

> *"Now the law came in so that trespass*
> *might increase. But where sin*
> *increased, grace increased all the*
> *more, so that just as sin ruled in death,*
> *so also grace might rule through*
> *righteousness, leading to eternal life*
> *through Jesus Christ our Lord."*
>
> —*Romans 5:20–21*

Grace reigns.

Not sin.

Not performance.

Not hustle.

Grace.

When a Missed Devotional Feels Like Failure

Elena's breaking point came one afternoon when she forgot to do her devotional.

Just forgot.

No rebellion. No laziness. Just life — a chaotic morning, a sick kid, a late start.

And the guilt hit her like a wave.

She felt like she had failed God.

Like the whole week was shot.

Like she wasn't even a "real Christian" anymore.

She almost didn't pray that night — not because she didn't believe, but because she didn't feel worthy.

And that's when it hit her.

She had built her spiritual life around herself — her discipline, her quiet time, her record.

It wasn't Jesus she was trusting. It was her consistency.

She didn't need more grit.

She needed more grace.

Jesus Meets Need, Not Performance
You know what's stunning about Jesus?

He never once scolded someone for needing grace.

He rebuked pride, yes.

He exposed hypocrisy.

He challenged apathy.

But the people who were most broken — most dependent — most unworthy?

He welcomed them.

He touched lepers.

He wept with mourners.

He defended the woman caught in adultery.

He dined with traitors.

And when Peter failed Him, denied Him, cursed and ran—Jesus cooked him breakfast and asked him to feed His sheep.

Not because Peter had proven himself.

But because Jesus had already decided that grace would be the foundation of the church.

Grace as Fuel, Not KPI
We think grit builds the kingdom.

But it doesn't.

Grace does.

Grace is the reason you're forgiven.

Grace is the reason you can change.

Grace is the reason you wake up and believe again after another failure.

Grace is the reason God isn't done with you yet.

And grace will be the reason you stand before Him one day—not with a résumé, but with a heart that knows:

I didn't earn this.

I didn't maintain this.

I received this.

> *"From his fullness we have all received grace upon grace."*
>
> *—John 1:16*

That's the gospel.

Not grit upon grit.

But grace upon grace.

What happens when grace becomes your fuel?

You stop needing to impress.

You start telling the truth.

You stop obsessing over outcomes.

You start walking in peace.

You stop comparing your spiritual walk to everyone else's.

You start resting in your Father's delight.

You stop seeing sin as a failure of willpower.

You start seeing it as a place where grace still wants to work.

From Routine to Relationship

Elena began rewriting her spiritual routines. Not abandoning them — but reorienting them.

No more rushing through chapters just to check a box.

No more shame when a day didn't go perfectly.

No more stacking disciplines to prove she was growing.

She started each morning not with goals, but with this prayer:

"God, remind me that You are the One holding me today. I receive Your grace again. Help me walk in it, not earn it."

That prayer changed everything.

She still read, still served, still gave — but now from a place of joy, not fear.

From fullness, not emptiness.

From identity, not insecurity.

Grace had stopped being an idea and become her reality.

He Will Do It

Maybe you're like Elena.

Maybe your walk with God feels more like a job than a joy.

Maybe your spiritual life is a cycle of zeal and burnout.

Maybe you feel closer to God when you're consistent, and distant when you fail — not because God moved, but because shame built a wall.

Maybe you've been running on grit for so long that you've forgotten how to receive.

Let grace interrupt your rhythm.

Let grace dismantle your performance.

Let grace remind you: this was never about you getting it all right.

It was always about Jesus doing what you never could.

> *"He who calls you is faithful;*
> *he will do it."*
>
> *—1 Thessalonians 5:24*

He will do it.

Not you.

Not your routines.

Not your willpower.

He.

Will.

Do it.

Because He is grace — and grace finishes what it starts.

So What…

Stop performing.

Start receiving.

Stop striving.

Start trusting.
Stop grading yourself on your spiritual output.

Start abiding in Christ.

Grit will give out.

Grace never will.

And when grace fuels your life, everything changes.

Not because you're strong.

But because He is.

7. How God Transforms What You Can't
It's Not About Turning Over a New Leaf—It's About Becoming a New Creation

There is a moment in every honest Christian's life when the mirror becomes unbearable.

The patterns you swore you'd break still echo in your life. The sin you claimed victory over creeps back in. You make the same promises again—I'll do better, I'll try harder, I won't fail this time—only to find yourself staring at the same version of you as before, but wearier now. More cynical. Less convinced that change is even possible.

It's a hollowing experience. When you've read the books, gone to the conferences, prayed the prayers, fasted, journaled, confessed, committed—when you've done all the "right" things but still find yourself stuck, something breaks. Not just hope. Identity.

You stop believing that transformation is for people like you.

That's the precise place God begins to work.

Because transformation was never going to come through your effort in the first place.

Not a Ladder, But a Life
In church, we talk a lot about sanctification. It's the lifelong process of becoming more like Christ. But often, we define that process with tools from the world of self-help. We talk about strategies. Habits. Mindset. We tell people to "do the work," "get serious," and "fight the flesh." We treat spiritual

maturity like a ladder—one we climb higher with enough grit, discipline, and spiritual hustle.

And to be fair, the desire to grow is good. The discipline matters. The will to obey is essential. But if the process depends on us, we're doomed before we begin.

Paul made this point unmistakably clear to the Philippians:

> *"Therefore, my beloved, just as you have always obeyed—not only in my presence, but now even more in my absence—work out your own salvation with fear and trembling. For it is God who is working in you both to will and to work for his good purpose."*

> *—Philippians 2:12–13*

Look closely at the tension. You're called to engage. "Work out your salvation." You are not passive. But then Paul immediately corrects the source: *It is God who is working in you.*

Not beside you. Not after you. **In** you.

The same God who saved you is actively at work within you—not only empowering the action, but shaping the desire.

You are not the source of your own transformation.

The Failure of the Bootstrap Gospel
This flies in the face of what most of us were taught to believe. Especially those of us raised with the bootstrap gospel. The unspoken message was simple: God saved you—now it's your job not to blow it. The Spirit got you in the door, but it's up

to you to stay faithful. You better fight the good fight. You better not slip. You better not be one of the ones who fall away.

The fear was holy-sounding. The anxiety was dressed up as seriousness. And the pride of self-discipline was mistaken for godliness.

But what it produced was not lasting joy. It was pressure. Performance. Fear.

And beneath it all, quiet despair.

Because the truth is—none of us can transform ourselves.

You can educate your mind.

You can alter your behavior.

You can clean up your vocabulary, attend services, install filters, and set boundaries.

But you cannot change your heart.

Only God can do that.

God Promised to Do It
This is why God promised, centuries before Jesus came, to do a work in His people that no law could ever accomplish.

Through Ezekiel, He declared:

> *"I will give you a new heart and put a*
> *new spirit in you.*
>
> *I will take away your heart of stone and*
> *give you a heart of flesh.*
>
> *I will put my Spirit in you and move*
> *you to follow my commands and be*
> *careful to do what I say."*
>
> *—Ezekiel 36:26–27*

This is not poetic metaphor. It's a promise of supernatural transformation.

Notice the subject: *I will... I will... I will...*

The action belongs to God.

The work of deep transformation—the kind that reshapes desires, restores affections, and uproots decades of sin-worn grooves in the heart—is divine.

You are not the artist.

You are the canvas.

Peter's Transformation Wasn't Performance
To understand the difference between self-effort and Spirit-empowered transformation, look at the life of Peter.

Before the cross, Peter was all grit. All declarations. He was the first to speak, the first to act, the first to swear allegiance. "Even if all fall away," he said, "I never will."

And then he did.

Three times.

To a servant girl.

Peter's betrayal wasn't just a moral failure—it was a soul collapse. His pride died that night. His boldness shattered. His confidence dissolved in tears outside the courtyard.

But Jesus had already seen it coming.

And He already planned Peter's restoration.

After the resurrection, Jesus doesn't berate him. He doesn't hand him a worksheet of goals or give him a twelve-step program. He cooks him breakfast. Then He asks a simple, piercing question: "Do you love Me?"

Three times, to match the denials.

And each time, Peter answers yes.

Jesus replies, "Feed My sheep."

That's grace.

That's transformation.

Not guilt-driven reform.

But love-led renewal.

By the time we get to Acts, Peter is unrecognizable. Bold again—but not boastful. Courageous—but not impulsive. Broken—but deeply usable.

He's not trying to prove himself anymore. He's simply being who Jesus has remade him to be.

Because that's what transformation looks like.

It's not you working harder.

It's God working deeper.

The Two Ditches of Self-Effort

When we confuse effort with transformation, we either become prideful or paralyzed.

Prideful, when our disciplines seem to be "working." We pray more, study more, sin less—so we start to believe that we've matured ourselves. We subtly assume we're better than others. We lose compassion. We forget that it is *only* by grace we've grown at all.

Or paralyzed, when the old habits don't break. When the temptations keep whispering. When the anger still bubbles, the bitterness still flares, the lust still circles like a vulture. We start to believe we're hopeless. That we must not be trying hard enough. That maybe we're just not cut out for this kind of life.

But both responses are rooted in the same lie: that **you** are the one who changes you.

You're not.

God is.

What Abiding Really Means

That doesn't mean you do nothing. It means you do the right thing—the only thing that can actually bear fruit: **abide**.

> *"Remain in Me, and I will remain in you. Just as a branch cannot bear fruit by itself unless it remains in the vine, neither can you unless you remain in me. I am the vine; you are the branches. The one who remains in me and I in him bears much fruit, for apart from me, you can do nothing."*
>
> *—John 15:4–5*

Abiding is not passive.

It's not laziness.

It's not waiting around for God to zap you into holiness.

Abiding is the active, daily posture of remaining connected to Jesus—through His Word, through prayer, through honesty, through worship, through dependency.

It's waking up and saying, *I cannot change myself. But I will remain in You, and trust that You are changing me.*

Real Transformation Takes Time

That's what makes transformation so hard for the self-help generation. We want control. We want to track our progress.

We want to read the charts and measure the wins. We want to know if we're ahead of schedule. We want to be able to say, "I did that."

But the Spirit doesn't work on a spreadsheet.

He works in secret places. In slow seasons. In unseen roots.

He is forming Christ in you—whether you feel it or not.

You don't measure this by behavior alone. You measure it by fruit: love, joy, peace, patience, kindness, goodness, faithfulness, gentleness, self-control.

And fruit takes time.

No tree produces overnight.

No soul becomes like Christ in a week.

The Encouragement and the Warning
That's the encouragement and the warning.

The encouragement: You don't have to produce what you cannot. God is at work, and He will finish what He started.

The warning: You can't fake the fruit. You can't substitute religious activity for spiritual formation. You can attend church, lead a group, quote Scripture, and still be disconnected from the Vine.

God is not looking for activity.

He's looking for surrender.

Because surrender is the soil where transformation takes root.

A Story of Transformation: David
There's a man in our congregation—David—who spent thirty years trying to fix himself.

He struggled with addiction in his youth, kicked it, got married, had kids, but the patterns never really left. They just went underground. His discipline kept things respectable. But the anger, the shame, the desire to hide—it remained.

He came to us burned out. "I've tried everything," he said. "Accountability. Fasting. Counseling. I've gone to conferences, I've read every book. I can white-knuckle my way through for a while, but it always comes back."

We didn't give him a new plan.

We gave him the gospel.

Again.

We taught him to sit with God.

To read without rushing.

To pray without pretending.

To confess without performing.

To receive the love of Christ without trying to "feel it."

To rest.

It took time.

But slowly, something shifted. Not just behavior. Identity.

He stopped asking "Am I enough yet?"

And started believing "Christ is enough for me."

That's when transformation began.

How Real Change Happens
We don't change by trying harder.

We change by trusting deeper.

We change when we stop treating the Spirit like a personal trainer and start honoring Him as Lord.

We change when we let the Word of God dwell in us richly—not just as information, but as nourishment.

We change when we let go of the fear that we'll never be different—and lean into the truth that the One who began this work *will complete it.*

> *"And we all, who with unveiled faces,*
> *contemplate the Lord's glory, are*
> *being transformed into his image with*
> *ever increasing glory, which comes*
> *from the Lord, who is the Spirit."*
>
> *—2 Corinthians 3:18*

This is not a motivational cycle. It's a miraculous work.

Not a self-improvement program. A supernatural process.

God does not patch up your old self.

He crucifies it.

And raises up a new creation in Christ.

So What...

Stop trying to change yourself.

Start surrendering yourself.

Lay down your strategies.

Lean into the Spirit.

Don't measure your growth by how you feel today.

Measure it by whether or not you're staying connected to the One who is growing you.

He is faithful.

He is working.

And He will not stop.

Not until the day He finishes what you never could.

8. Resting in a Power Greater Than You
The Power Was Never Yours to Begin With

Not long ago, I sat across from a man who hadn't taken a full day off in five years. No vacations. No sabbath. No breaks. Just work. Good work, even. He was a ministry leader, married, kids, running a growing business. He loved Jesus, gave generously, served his church, read the Bible every morning. But his hands shook slightly as he talked, and when I asked when he last felt peace—real peace—he said, "I don't remember."

He wasn't sinning in some scandalous way. He wasn't rebelling against God. But he was exhausted—and proud of it. Somewhere along the way, he had absorbed the idea that *rest is for the weak.* That stopping means you're falling behind. That unless you're grinding, someone else is gaining. That God might love you, but He sure expects results.

He looked me in the eye and said what so many Christians feel but rarely admit:

> *"I trust God. But I feel like it's all on me."*

That one sentence holds the root of burnout. The illusion that even though God is good, He still needs you to keep everything running. That your family, your church, your business, your finances, your spiritual walk—somehow all depend on your endless effort.

It's a lie. A deeply spiritual, highly praised, culturally reinforced lie.

But it is a lie nonetheless.

And the only cure is rest. Not a nap. Not a weekend getaway. But a deep, soul-level rest that flows from knowing that **you are not the power that sustains your life.**

Rest is a Gift, Not a Reward

Jesus didn't call the weary to work harder. He didn't shout at the burned out. He didn't guilt the overwhelmed. He gave an invitation:

> *"Come to Me, all you who are weary and burdened, and I will give you rest. Take My yoke upon you and learn from Me, because I am gentle and humble in heart, and you will find rest for your souls. For My yoke is easy, and my burden is light."*
>
> *—Matthew 11:28–30*

Notice who He calls: not the strong, but the weary. Not the capable, but the burdened. And what does He offer? Not more strength. Not better time management. Not divine productivity hacks.

He offers rest.

Not as a reward for your effort.

As a gift for your surrender.

The Danger of Self-Reliance

Many of us never experience this rest—not because God is withholding it, but because we are too determined to stay in control.

We don't like surrender. We like solving problems. We like being dependable. We like being the one others look to. We fear what might happen if we stop carrying the weight.

What will happen if we don't show up?

If we don't say yes?

If we don't hold it all together?

So we tighten our grip, smile through the stress, and keep going—until something breaks.

Maybe your health. Maybe your marriage. Maybe your walk with God.

But make no mistake: *relentless self-reliance always costs more than we expect.*

It erodes intimacy. It masks fear. And it slowly replaces grace with pressure.

Scripture is filled with God's consistent reminder: **You are not your own source.**

Stillness is Strength

One of the most striking moments in the Old Testament happens not in a battle, but in a command.

> *"For the Lord GOD, the Holy One of*
> *Israel, has said: 'In repentance and rest*
> *you will be saved; In quietness and trust is*
> *your strength.' But you were not willing."*

—*Isaiah 30:15*

God offered His people rest.

He offered strength through stillness.

But they refused.
They preferred to mount up, to ride fast horses, to outrun their enemies. They chose movement over dependence.

And God let them run—right into collapse.

How many times have we done the same?

We feel the pressure. We see the threat. And instead of returning to the quiet presence of God, we double down on our own resolve.

We don't say it out loud, but the message is clear: *I'll fix this.*

God doesn't need your hustle. He wants your heart. He doesn't bless your frantic striving. He blesses your quiet trust.

Rest is Worship
Rest is not weakness. It is worship.

It is the declaration that **God is enough**—even when you aren't.

The psalmist knew this well:

> *"Be still, and know that I am God. I*
> *will be exalted among the nations; I*
> *will be exalted in the earth."*
>
> *—Psalm 46:10*

This wasn't a whisper at a spa. It was a war psalm.

Nations rage. Kingdoms totter. The earth trembles.

And in the middle of chaos, God says, *Be still.*

Still—not because everything is calm.

Still—because you know He is God, and you are not.

Sabbath Was God's Idea

We live in a culture that praises the over functioning. We reward busyness. We admire those who grind. We brand exhaustion as virtue. We equate rest with laziness, margin with weakness.

But Sabbath was God's idea, not man's.

In Exodus 20, God commands His people to rest—not as an afterthought, but as a holy rhythm.

> *"Remember the Sabbath day, to set it*
> *apart. You are to labor six days and do*
> *all your work, but the seventh day is a*
> *Sabbath to the LORD your God. You*
> *must not do any work..."*
>
> *—Exodus 20:8–10*

This was more than just physical recovery. It was theological training.

Every week, the people of God laid down their tools to declare: *God provides. God governs. God is our source.*

The Sabbath taught them that **rest is an act of faith**.

That's still true today.

Rest Exposes Idols

When you stop—truly stop—you declare that the world does not rise and fall on your output.

You admit that your identity is not wrapped in your productivity.

You trust that God is capable of doing more through your surrender than through your striving.

But rest is hard.

It exposes us.

It surfaces our idols.

It reveals whether we truly trust God's sufficiency or not.

One of the clearest signs that you're running on your own strength is the inability to stop.

Even for an hour.

Even for a day.

Even with your phone turned off.

Even with the inbox untouched.

If silence terrifies you… if margin feels like failure… if slowing down feels dangerous… your soul is not at rest.

You are being powered by your flesh—even if your intentions are noble.

And flesh, no matter how religious it looks, eventually fails.

Jesus Modeled Rest

Jesus modeled rest not because He needed it, but because we do.

He withdrew often.

He stepped away from the crowds.

He said no to good things so He could stay aligned with His Father.

He slept in storms.

He walked instead of ran.

He didn't heal every disease or answer every question or calm every fear.

Because Jesus wasn't driven by need.

He was led by trust.

If the Son of God could rest—amid crisis, demand, and expectation—why can't we?

Because we still believe the lie: *If I stop, it will all fall apart.*

But here's the truth:

If it falls apart when you rest, it was never held together by God.

It was held together by your fear.

The Lesson of Manna

When the Israelites gathered manna in the wilderness, God instructed them to collect only what they needed for each day—except before the Sabbath. On the sixth day, they gathered twice as much, and miraculously, it didn't spoil.

God was teaching them not just provision, but trust.

He was saying, *I can do more with your six days than you can do with seven.*
But some people disobeyed. They tried to hoard. They feared lack. They didn't rest.

And the manna rotted.

We do the same when we refuse to rest. We hoard our energy. We refuse to trust. We try to get ahead. And our joy spoils. Our health rots. Our relationships suffer.

Because we never learned the spiritual discipline of stopping.

Rest is Resistance

Rest is not a luxury.

It is resistance.

It resists the tyranny of performance.

It resists the idol of productivity.

It resists the lie that you are your own provider.

It trains your heart to trust the God who never sleeps.

Weakness is an Invitation

If you've lived long enough, you've likely had your strength fail.

Not because you were bad—but because you're human. Maybe it was physical burnout. Maybe emotional collapse. Maybe moral failure. Or maybe just spiritual emptiness that lingered longer than it should.

Whatever the case, you came to the end of your strength.

That's not a failure.

That's an invitation.

The apostle Paul described a season like this in 2 Corinthians. He was afflicted. Overwhelmed. Pressed beyond his ability to endure. But through that breaking came revelation:

> *"Indeed, we felt that we had received the sentence of death. But that was to make us rely not on ourselves but on God, who raises the dead."*

—*2 Corinthians 1:9*

Paul wasn't ashamed of his weakness.

He understood it.

God had let his strength collapse—not to punish him, but to teach him *who the real power was.*

You don't need to be stronger.

You need to stop pretending you are.

Spiritual Maturity Looks Like Surrender

Spiritual maturity doesn't look like unbreakable endurance.

It looks like quick surrender.

The faster you collapse into grace, the longer you'll last.

The sooner you rest in His power, the less you'll need to prove your own.

The Risk of a Full Calendar

In my own life, rest is often the first thing to go when I feel pressure. My brain speeds up. My calendar fills. I respond faster. I pray less. I plan more.

But I've learned the hard way that a life without margin is a life without listening.

When I rush, I stop hearing God.

When I overcommit, I miss His presence.

When I power through, I lose the peace that anchors me.

So I've had to learn—and am still learning—that my effectiveness is not measured by how much I do, but by how deeply I stay connected to the One who empowers me.

So What...
Where is God calling you to rest?

Not just physically—but spiritually, emotionally, mentally?

Where have you been shouldering a weight He never asked you to carry?

Where have you exchanged dependence for pride?

Maybe it's time to block off a day.

Maybe it's time to say no to the good thing.

Maybe it's time to cancel the commitment that's draining you dry.

Maybe it's time to stop "doing more" and start trusting deeper.

You are not the power source.

You were never meant to be.

Let go.

Be still.

Receive the rest that only Jesus gives.

And in that quiet place, you will remember:

He is God.

You are not.

And that is very good news.

9. You Don't Have to Fix Yourself
Jesus Didn't Come to Improve You—He Came to Make You New

A young woman once sat across from me, shoulders tight, hands locked together in her lap, and said with trembling frustration: "I know God loves me... I just don't think He likes me very much."

I asked her why. She started listing things: her past, her temper, the way she kept messing up with her boyfriend, the promises she kept breaking. She was praying more, reading Scripture daily, journaling her struggles, but she still felt broken. She couldn't forgive herself, and she was sure God hadn't either.

What stood out most wasn't her sin. It was her exhaustion. She had been trying to fix herself. Trying to repent better. Trying to be humbler. Trying to stop disappointing God. And she was worn out. Not from rebellion—but from effort.

And what broke my heart most was that she thought that's what God wanted from her.

The Futility of Self-Fixing
We live in an age obsessed with self-fixing. It's not just a cultural trend—it's a religious reflex. We assume that if something is wrong in us, it's our job to make it right. If we fall short, we should work harder. If we sin, we should atone. If we're not growing, we must be doing something wrong.

We love grace in theory.

But when it comes down to how we treat ourselves—or how we imagine God treats us—most of us default to works.

We believe that God helps those who help themselves. That change depends on our discipline. That healing comes after enough sorrow. That forgiveness is available, but only to the truly remorseful.

So we keep trying to fix ourselves—cleaning up just enough to feel like maybe we deserve to be near God again. But the closer we get, the more our flaws show. And we start again. Trying harder. Repenting deeper. Hoping someday we'll be different.

But the truth is:

You don't need to fix yourself. You can't.

And you were never asked to.

Grace Starts—and Stays—with God

The gospel does not begin with *what you must do.*

It begins with what **God has already done**.

Paul writes it plainly:

> *"But God demonstrates his own love*
> *for us in this: While we were still*
> *sinners, Christ died for us."*
>
> *—Romans 5:8*

Not *after* you got your act together.

Not *once* you showed real progress.

While you were still in sin.

God's love met you in your worst condition—not your best.

Jesus didn't die for your cleaned-up version. He died for the real you—the one you're still ashamed of. The one you're still trying to fix.

Love First, Change Second

That means you don't have to clean yourself up to come to Jesus.

You come filthy, and He makes you clean.

You come broken, and He makes you whole.

You come empty, and He fills you.

You come sinful, and He makes you righteous.

This isn't poetry.

It's theology.

It's the foundation of grace.

When Effort Sneaks Back In

In *Self Help* religion, change is the condition for love.

In the gospel, love is the condition for change.

When Paul wrote to the believers in Galatia, he was livid—not because they rejected Jesus, but because they were trying to *add* to Him.

They had started by trusting Christ, but then returned to the law. They believed they needed to *complete* their salvation through effort, through circumcision, through obedience to the old covenant. They thought Jesus was the starting line—but they would have to finish the race themselves.

Paul rebukes them sharply:

> *"Are you so foolish? After beginning by the Spirit, are you now finishing in the flesh?"*

> *—Galatians 3:3*

This is the same trap we fall into today.

We start by grace—and end in striving.

We receive salvation as a gift—and try to maintain it as a wage.

We sing "Jesus paid it all"—and live like we're paying Him back.
But that's not the gospel.

That's religion dressed up as discipleship.

"It Is Finished" Means Finished

When Jesus cried, *"It is finished,"* on the cross, He wasn't talking about a partial down payment.

He was declaring your debt fully satisfied.

The record of your sin erased.

The wrath you deserved absorbed.

The shame you carried canceled.

And the righteousness you needed given—freely, fully, forever.

Paul put it this way:

> *"But God, who is rich in mercy,*
> *because of his great love that he had*
> *for us, made us alive with Christ even*
> *though we were dead in trespasses.*
> *You are saved by grace! He also raised*
> *us up with him and seated us with him*
> *in the heavenly places in Christ Jesus."*
>
> *—Ephesians 2:4–6,*

You were dead—not wounded, not weak. Dead.

And God made you alive—not by reforming you, not by improving you, not by helping you help yourself—but by raising you through Jesus.

That's not self-help.

That's resurrection.

Grace Offends Our Pride
Still, we struggle to receive it.

Because grace insults our pride.

We want to contribute something. To earn it. To feel like we had a hand in our healing.

But if you had to fix yourself before God loved you, it would mean that His love was conditional.

And if His love is conditional, it's not love. It's transaction.

But God's love is not a paycheck.

It's not a prize for performance.

It's a gift for the unworthy.

The Tax Collector Went Home Justified

There's a story Jesus told that still offends religious people today. A Pharisee and a tax collector go up to the temple to pray (Luke 18). One thanks God that he's righteous, tithes, fasts, obeys the rules. The other beats his chest, won't even look up, and prays, *"God, have mercy on me, a sinner."*

Jesus says only one man went home justified.

And it wasn't the one trying to prove he was good enough. It was the one who knew he wasn't—and trusted God anyway.

Grace Changes Everything

You don't get clean and come to God.

You come to God and He makes you clean.

You don't prove yourself and receive grace.

You receive grace, and it changes everything.

You're Carried Out, Not Climbing Out
There's an old story of a man who fell into a pit. He tried climbing out, digging steps, calling for help. A philosopher walked by and gave him a lecture. A religious leader told him to meditate. A friend tossed him a rope—but not far enough. Then Jesus came by, climbed into the pit, and carried him out.

That's the gospel.

You don't climb out.

You're carried out.
You don't fix yourself.

You fall into grace.

Grace Doesn't Excuse Sin—It Heals It
And yet—this isn't permission to stay in sin.

Grace doesn't ignore your brokenness.

It heals it.

Grace doesn't make sin irrelevant.

It makes it powerless.

Paul asked the very question we're all tempted to ask:

> *"What should we say then? Should we
> keep on sinning so that grace may*

*increase? Absolutely not! Since we who
died to sin how can we still live in it?"*

—*Romans 6:1–2*

Grace changes us—but not by demanding we fix ourselves.

It changes us from the inside out.

Love First, Then Obedience

Transformation is real. Obedience matters. Holiness is beautiful.

But all of it is downstream from love.

You don't obey to get God's approval.

You obey because you already have it.

You don't strive to earn grace.

You surrender to be changed by it.

What to Do When You Feel Broken

So what do you do when you feel broken?

When your failures pile up?

When you're tired of apologizing?

You run—not away from God, but to Him.

You collapse into the truth.

You remind your soul:

I am not the solution.

Jesus is.

I am not the fixer.

Jesus is.

I am not the foundation.
Jesus is.

Come As You Are
God isn't waiting for the better version of you.

He sees you now—and loves you now.

He is not asking you to repair yourself before you belong.

He is inviting you to rest in the One who already finished the work.

So What...
Stop trying to be your own savior.

Stop managing your sin like it's a project.

Stop measuring your worth by your spiritual performance.

You don't need a better strategy.

You need a deeper surrender.

You don't need to fix yourself.

You need to believe that Jesus really does.

Come to Him—not when you're cleaned up.

Come now.

Come messy.

Come ashamed.

Come weary.

Come stubborn.

And let grace do what you never could.

10. Grace That Works When You Can't
The Power of God Is Perfected in Weakness—Not Willpower

He didn't look like a man on the edge. Nice clothes. Clean shave. The kind of smile you wear when you've practiced it. He was a father of four, a deacon at his church, a project manager at a company that paid him well and demanded more. But behind that tired grin was a man who had been treading water for too long.

He told me that morning, "I'm doing everything I'm supposed to. But I'm sinking."

It wasn't scandal. No affair. No secret addiction. Just the slow erosion of trying to do everything right and still feeling like he was coming up short. He was praying daily, serving faithfully, reading his Bible. But every effort seemed to be met with silence, heaviness, and exhaustion.

"I thought if I stayed disciplined, if I showed up, if I kept pushing — it would all get better," he said. "But I'm tired. I'm not okay. And I don't know how to fix it."

And that's when I told him something most people in churches never hear.

"You can't fix it. And God never asked you to."

When Strength Becomes a Burden
We don't notice it at first — the weight of having to hold everything together. It creeps in gradually, disguised as responsibility. Especially if you've grown up in church, you learn early that God is pleased with obedience, hard work, and

sacrifice. So you try. You take on more. You work on your attitude. You keep smiling. And it works… until it doesn't.

Eventually, your performance starts to crack under the weight of your own humanity. You lose your patience with your spouse. You snap at your kids. You struggle to find time to pray. And guilt sets in — not just because of what you've done, but because you should've known better. You should be stronger than this. More mature. More consistent.

So what do you do? You try harder.

You double down on the plan. You add another Bible reading goal. You wake up earlier. You say yes to more ministry. You hold yourself together — even if it's only with duct tape and willpower.

But behind the scenes, your soul is fraying.

This is the great lie of self-powered faith: that your grit can accomplish what only grace was meant to do.

The Apostle Paul's Thorn

Paul was no spiritual lightweight. If anyone had the right to boast about spiritual maturity, it was him. He was a scholar, a missionary, a miracle-worker, a martyr-in-training. And yet, even Paul faced something in his life he could not conquer — something he called his "thorn in the flesh."

We're never told exactly what it was. Physical illness? A mental battle? A spiritual torment? Scholars debate it, but Paul only tells us that it was painful, persistent, and humiliating. He pleaded with God — not once, but three times — to take it away.

And God said no.

But He didn't leave Paul alone. He gave him something far better than instant relief.

> *"But he said to me, 'My grace is*
> *sufficient for you, for my power is*
> *made perfect in weakness.' Therefore I*
> *will boast all the more gladly of my*
> *weaknesses, so that the power of*
> *Christ may rest over me."*
>
> *—2 Corinthians 12:9*

God didn't offer Paul a strategy. He offered him **sufficiency**.

Grace is More Than Forgiveness

Let's clear something up: grace isn't just the eraser that wipes away your past. It's the power that carries you forward.

Paul didn't say, *"I'm okay with my weakness because God will forgive me later."* He said, *"I will boast in it — because that's where Christ's power shows up."*

This is grace as power. Grace that steps in when strength runs out. Grace that holds your mind together when your thoughts betray you. Grace that lifts your heart when depression won't budge. Grace that says, "You're mine," when shame says, "You're done."

And this kind of grace doesn't come through effort. It comes through **abiding**.

The Vine and the Branches

Jesus used a metaphor in John 15 that every disciple needs burned into their bones:

> *"I am the vine; you are the branches.*
> *The one who remains in me, and I in*
> *him, bears much fruit, for apart from*
> *me, you can do nothing."*
>
> *—John 15:5*

Branches don't work hard to produce fruit. They stay connected. They draw life from the vine. The moment they disconnect — even if they still look good for a while — they begin to wither.

The fruit you long for — patience, joy, peace, faithfulness — doesn't come from grit. It comes from grace. And grace comes through staying close to Jesus.

Abiding is not laziness. It's spiritual surrender. It's the refusal to white-knuckle your way through another spiritual task list. It's the steady, daily reliance on Jesus for what you cannot produce on your own.

Stop Trying to Impress God

Some of us are not fighting sin so much as we're fighting grace.

We'd rather God be proud of us than be near to us.

We'd rather earn His approval than fall into His arms.

We'd rather get better than get honest.

But grace only flows where there is humility. And humility begins when you admit the truth: You're not enough. You weren't meant to be. And you don't have to be.

God is not impressed with your consistency. He's not waiting for your best day. He's not marking your chart for gold stars.

He's looking for surrender.

The Spirit That Works in You

Paul writes something astounding in Philippians 2. After telling believers to "work out your salvation with fear and trembling," he immediately explains what that looks like:

> *"For it is God who is working in you, both to will and to work for His good pleasure."*

> *—Philippians 2:13*

Read that again. It's **God** working in you — both the desire and the ability.

You can't even want the right things without Him.

That's how deep your need is. And that's how complete His provision is.

You don't just need grace to forgive you.

You need grace to want Him.

You need grace to obey.

You need grace to love your enemy.

You need grace to keep showing up when you're unseen, unthanked, unappreciated.

And that grace is already yours — if you'll stop trying to earn what you've already been given.

When the Bottom Falls Out
I've met people who didn't meet grace until they lost everything.

The job they built their life on collapsed. The marriage they thought would hold cracked under pressure. The faith they wore like armor suddenly couldn't shield them anymore.

And in that collapse — when their strategies failed, when their wisdom proved inadequate, when their best efforts couldn't bring relief — they met Jesus.

Not the distant God they tried to impress.

The near God who climbed into the pit with them.

The Savior who doesn't demand we climb, but carries us.

The Power That Holds You
Romans 8 says something staggering:

> *"In the same way, the Spirit helps us in*
> *our weakness. For we do not know*
> *what to pray for as we should, but the*
> *Spirit Himself intercedes for us with*
> *groanings too deep for words."*

> *—Romans 8:26*

Not only does God forgive your weakness.

He speaks for you when you're too weak to form the words.

That's grace.

Grace that steps in when you don't know how to pray.

Grace that lifts your hands when they're trembling.

Grace that holds you fast when you can't hold on.

So What...
Are you tired of pushing?

Of performing?

Of hiding how much you're hurting?

What if this is the moment to let go — not into apathy, but into grace?

What if the greatest spiritual breakthrough of your life isn't on the other side of effort...

...but on the other side of surrender?

You're not a project God is waiting to see completed.

You're a child He already calls beloved.

You don't have to prove anything. You don't have to earn what's already yours. You don't have to fake strength.

You only have to stay close.

So fall into the vine. Let the branch be the branch.

Let grace do what you can't.

And rest in the power that works when you can't.

11. You Can't Go Back — But You Can Be Made New
Why You Don't Have to Fix It First

She stood in the doorway of the church lobby, staring at the sanctuary like it was a crime scene.

It had been twelve years since she walked through those doors. Twelve years since the abortion. Since the divorce. Since she got tired of pretending her faith was stronger than her pain. The church had sent casseroles when her father died. But they didn't know what to do when she started asking questions. When she stopped showing up. When she stopped wearing the right face.

Now here she was — older, fragile, heavier in spirit than she ever imagined. A single mom, recovering addict, holding onto the fraying thread of hope that maybe, just maybe, God still wanted her.

The hardest step wasn't getting to the parking lot. It wasn't turning off the engine. It wasn't even opening the front doors.

The hardest step was walking in like she belonged.

The Pull of the Past
We all have places we can't go back to. Not physically — spiritually.

That moment when we crossed a line. The day we said it. The night we did it. The person we used to be.

Regret is a heavy backpack. It whispers, *"If only."* If only I had stayed. If only I had spoken up. If only I had never met them. If only I had said no.

And shame — shame comes with an even sharper edge.

Not just *"I did wrong,"* but *"I am wrong."*

So we live in this tension: We long for freedom, but we're haunted by who we were.

And sometimes we believe the lie that because we can't go back, we can't go forward.

The Lie of Irreparable Damage
Some people stay away from God not because they don't believe He's real, but because they believe they've ruined the chance to be loved by Him.

They think grace has an expiration date. That God might forgive *others*, but surely not *them*.

But Jesus tells a different story.

> *"Then he said, a man had two sons.*
> *The younger one said to his father,*
> *'Father, give me my share of the*
> *estate.' So he divided his property*
> *between them."*
>
> *—Luke 15:11–12*

We call it the story of the Prodigal Son. But it's really the story of the Prodigal Father — the one who gave recklessly. The one who ran shamelessly. The one who embraced a ruined son and wouldn't let him finish his apology.

> *"So he got up and went to his father.*
> *But while he was still far away, his*
> *father saw him and was filled with*
> *compassion. He ran, threw his arms*
> *around his neck, and kissed him."*

> —*Luke 15:20*

He didn't say, *"Let's talk about what you did."* He didn't say, *"Let's take it slow."* He didn't even say, *"I forgive you."*

He just ran. He just embraced. He just restored.

Grace Doesn't Rewind — It Rewrites

The father didn't take the son back to the beginning. He gave him a new start right where he stood.

That's what God does with broken people. He doesn't pretend your past didn't happen. He just refuses to let it define you.

> *"So if the Son sets you free,*
> *you really will be free."*

> —*John 8:36*

Not hypothetically free. Not marginally free. *Truly. Fully. Permanently.*

Jesus doesn't rewind your story. He redeems it.

The Myth of Going Back

When Peter betrayed Jesus, it wasn't a one-time slip. It was denial — repeated, emphatic, cowardly.

He didn't just fall. He folded.

Later, Jesus finds Peter on a beach. Peter had gone back to fishing. Back to what he knew. Back to the man he used to be.

Jesus doesn't scold him. He cooks him breakfast.

> *"Jesus came, took the bread, and gave it to them. He did the same with the fish."*
>
> *—John 21:13*

After they ate, Jesus didn't say, *"Why did you do it?"* He said, *"Do you love Me?"*

Three times — not to shame him, but to restore him.

Peter didn't get to undo the denial. He didn't get to pretend it didn't happen.

But he was still called. Still chosen. Still the rock on which the church would grow.

You can't go back to undo your worst moment. But God can meet you right in the wreckage and build something better.

Made New, Not Repaired
Christianity is not spiritual duct tape. It's death and resurrection.

God isn't in the business of patching up your old life. He gives you a new one.

> *"We were buried with Him through*
> *immersion into death, so that just as*
> *Christ was raised from the dead*
> *through the glory of the Father, we too*
> *can live a new life."*
>
> *—Romans 6:4*

You don't get your old self back, improved. You get a new self — born of the Spirit, alive to God.

This is why baptism is not just symbolic — it's seismic.

You're not just cleansed. You're reborn.

What About the Consequences?
But what about the mess I made?

That's real.

Sometimes the damage can't be reversed. The marriage is over. The child is estranged. The reputation is scarred. The opportunity is gone.

But here's what the gospel declares:

Even if you can't fix what's behind you, you are not chained to it.

God doesn't promise to erase the consequences — but He does promise to walk with you through them.

And sometimes the most powerful testimony is not that God kept you from the fire… but that He pulled you out of it and walked with you as the smoke cleared.

The Shame You Don't Have to Carry
Paul called himself the "worst of sinners." Not in theory — in reality. He had murdered believers. Torn families apart. Persecuted Jesus Himself.

But he didn't live under shame. He lived under grace.

> *"But by the grace of God I am what I am, and His grace toward me was not wasted. Instead, I worked harder than all of them—yet not I, but the grace of God that was with me."*

> *—1 Corinthians 15:10*

Paul knew he couldn't go back. But he also knew he wasn't who he used to be.

Grace didn't ignore his past. It just refused to let it define his future.

You Can Be Made New
One of the most powerful verses in the Bible says:

> *"Therefore, there is now no condemnation for those who are in Christ Jesus."*

> *—Romans 8:1*

Not *less* condemnation. Not *delayed* condemnation. *No condemnation.*

Not because you've been perfect. But because you've been made new.

You don't need to rehearse your failure. You don't need to explain yourself to earn God's kindness. You don't need to go back.

You just need to come.

So What...
Maybe you've been trying to go back.

Back to the version of you before it all broke. Back to the church before you got hurt. Back to the faith you used to have. Back to the marriage before the betrayal. Back to the innocence before the abuse.

But going back is not the gospel.

The gospel is this:

> *You can't go back.*
> *But you can be made new.*
> *Right here.*
> *Right now.*
> *In the arms of the One who never left.*

Let Him make you new.

12. What If I Try and Fail Again?
You're Not the Exception to Mercy

Jake sat across from me, fingers interlocked, jaw tight, voice low.

"I've promised God a hundred times. A thousand, maybe. Every time, I meant it. I meant it when I said I'd stop. Meant it when I swore I'd never look at that again. Meant it when I vowed to pray every morning, to be present with my family, to walk away from the bottle."

He stared down at his shoes.

"And I keep screwing it up. I'm starting to think maybe I'm the problem grace doesn't cover."

He didn't say it with arrogance. He said it like a man who had already condemned himself, long before God ever would. He believed in forgiveness — just not for himself. He believed in restoration — just not after this many chances. He believed in second chances — but not seventieth.

What do you say to someone who keeps trying... and keeps failing?

Maybe you already know what this chapter is about — not because you've read it before, but because you've lived it.

You know what it is to hate your own patterns. To vow to do better. To cry through an altar call. To mark a new beginning... and then blow it. Again.

And somewhere deep inside, you've asked the question:

What if I try... and fail again?

The Question We're Afraid to Ask
No one likes to talk about the "after." After you're immersed. After you're saved. After you commit. What happens when you mess up after all of that?

It's one thing to fall when you didn't know better. It's another thing to fall when you did.

The enemy loves to twist failure into identity.

You failed = You're a failure.
You sinned again = You never meant it before.
You blew it = You're not really saved.

That's how shame speaks — always personal, always final.

But shame doesn't get the last word.

Peter: The Apostle Who Blew It
Jesus warned Peter. "You're going to deny Me." Peter said, "Even if I have to die, I'll never deny You." (Matthew 26:35)

But when the moment came... He did exactly what he swore he wouldn't.

Not once. Not twice. Three times. Lied. Denied. Cursed.

> *Then the Lord turned and looked at*
> *Peter. And Peter remembered the word*

> *of the Lord, how he had said to him,*
> *"Before the rooster crows today, you*
> *will deny me three times." And he*
> *went outside and wept bitterly.*

> —*Luke 22:61–62*

Imagine that moment. Jesus doesn't say a word. He just *looks*.

And Peter crumbles.

The bravest disciple becomes the most broken.

The Look of Grace

But here's what matters most: That look from Jesus wasn't condemnation. It was grace.

Peter wept because he knew he failed someone who loved him. And that love would be what eventually restored him.

Later, after the resurrection, Jesus comes back — not to scold Peter, but to feed him.

He asks three questions — "Do you love Me?" — possibly one for each denial. He doesn't make Peter relive the failure. He leads him through redemption.

> *"Feed My sheep,"*
> *He says. "Follow Me."*

> —*John 21:17–19*

Jesus doesn't throw away people who fall again. He reinstates them. He uses them. He trusts them.

Even when they didn't trust themselves.

You're Not a Lost Cause

Paul once wrote:

> *"If we are faithless, he remains*
> *faithful, for he cannot deny Himself."*
>
> *—2 Timothy 2:13*

That verse is for the ones who blew it *after* they believed. For the ones who fell *after* they knew better. For the ones who wonder if God's grace has a limit.

And the answer is simple: **No.**

God is not finished with you because you failed. He's not disgusted with you. He's not withdrawing His Spirit. He's not tallying your stumbles with a frown and folded arms.

He is *faithful.*

Falling Doesn't Mean You're Fake

Somewhere along the line, we began equating struggle with hypocrisy.

We say, "I can't go back to church — I'm a mess." Or, "I don't want to pray until I get things right."

As if God is only interested in cleaned-up versions of us.

But He never asked you to fix yourself first. He asked you to come.

> *"Therefore, let us approach the throne*
> *of grace with boldness, so that we may*

> *receive mercy and find grace to help in*
> *time of need."*
>
> *—Hebrews 4:16*

You don't approach the throne once you've earned it. You approach it *in need.*

The Righteous Fall — And Rise Again

The Proverbs writer said:

> *"For though a righteous man falls*
> *seven times, he rises again, but the*
> *wicked stumble in times of disaster."*
>
> *—Proverbs 24:16*

Notice — he's still called "righteous" *even while falling.* Not because he's perfect, but because he keeps getting back up.

Grace doesn't mean you won't fall. It means you'll always have a hand reaching down to lift you again.

Every fall is an opportunity to believe the gospel all over again — that you're not accepted because you never sin… but because Jesus never stops saving.

You Can't Out-Sin the Cross

We don't say this flippantly. We don't excuse sin. But we do declare the truth:

You are not stronger than the cross.

Your sin isn't more powerful than Jesus' blood.

The lies you believed. The promises you broke. The things you said you'd never do again — but did. They are not too much for the grace of God.

> *"...But where sin increased, grace increased all the more."*
>
> *—Romans 5:20*

You can't outrun the mercy of God. You can't outlast His patience. You can't undo what Jesus finished.

What to Do After You Fall

1. **Don't hide.** Shame thrives in darkness. Bring it into the light — with God and with others.
2. **Don't fake it.** God's not impressed by your pretending. He's moved by your honesty.
3. **Confess.** Not to earn forgiveness — but to receive it.

> *"If we confess our sins, He is faithful and just to forgive us our sins and to cleanse us from all unrighteousness."*
>
> *—1 John 1:9*

4. **Get back up.** You're not finished. This isn't the end of your story.
5. **Walk forward — with God.** Not in fear, but in dependence. Not in pride, but in humility.

Jake's Story Isn't Over

Jake didn't leave that day fixed. He left heard. Known. Covered.

And slowly, things started to shift.

He stopped pretending he was stronger than he was. He stopped measuring himself by his last mistake. He stopped believing the lie that grace was only for first chances.

He started walking again. With scars. With accountability. With new rhythms.

And he started helping other men who were scared to try again.

Jake's story didn't end with failure. It started with grace.

Yours can, too.

So What...
So you've failed. So you've broken promises. So you've gone back to what you said you'd never touch again.

You're not disqualified. You're not discarded. You're not done.

You're exactly where grace does its best work.

The question isn't *"What if I fail again?"*

The better question is:

"What if God meets me again... and lifts me anyway?"

Because He will.

And He always has.

13. You Can Come Home Today
The Grace That Runs to Meet You

The night she came home, no one recognized her at first.

Her hair was matted. Her clothes hung off her frame. She smelled of the streets and something deeper — the smell of shame that clings to the soul like a second skin. She hadn't planned to come. She hadn't planned anything for a long time. But there she was, sitting in the back of the church during the second song, trying not to be seen, trying even harder not to bolt.

No one knew the last time she'd been in a pew, it was her father's funeral. No one knew she'd been living out of her car. No one knew she'd just whispered, "God, if You're real, help me."

But God knew.

And when the invitation song began, she broke. Not because the preacher was powerful. Not because the words were poetic. But because she couldn't run anymore. She didn't want to.

She just wanted to come home.

The Long Way Back
For some of us, the road away from God isn't sudden. It's not a dramatic rebellion. It's subtle.

You miss a Sunday. Then two. You stop praying, but tell yourself you'll get back to it. You start numbing — a drink here, a relationship there. Nothing evil, just enough to keep you from feeling empty.

Then one day you wake up and realize: You've wandered far, and you don't know how to get back.

Or worse — you wonder if God still wants you.

But let's be clear: **God always wants you.**

The Lie That Keeps You Gone

Shame says, "Not after all this time." Pride says, "You've got to fix it first." Fear says, "What if you mess up again?"

But the gospel says:

> *"I have wiped out your wrongdoings like a thick cloud And your sins like a heavy mist. Return to Me, for I have redeemed you."*
>
> *—Isaiah 44:22*

Not "Return once you've cleaned up." Not "Return when you can promise never to fail again." Just **return.**

You don't come home because you've earned it. You come home because God has already made the way.

The Invitation That Still Stands

Jesus once told a story about a father and a runaway.

The son didn't just leave — he demanded his inheritance, essentially saying, *"I wish you were dead."* He wasted it all on cheap pleasure. When the money ran out, the friends vanished. He ended up feeding pigs, hungry enough to eat their food.

That's when the memory hit him: *Even the servants in my father's house have it better than this. Maybe I can go back — not as a son, but as a servant.*

> *"So he got up and went to his father. But while he was still far away, his father saw him and was filled with compassion. He ran, threw his arms around his neck, and kissed him."*
>
> *—Luke 15:20*

The son tried to give his speech.

> *"The son said to him, 'Father, I have sinned against heaven and in your sight. I am no longer worthy to be called your son.'"*
>
> *—Luke 15:21*

But the father interrupted him.

> *"But the father told his servants, 'Quick! Bring out the best robe and put it on him. Put a ring on his finger and sandals on his feet. Bring the fattened calf and kill it. Let's celebrate with a feast,'"*
>
> *—Luke 15:22–23*

The son wanted to come back as a servant. The father received him as a son.

That's the gospel.

The Door Is Still Open

You may feel like you've burned the bridge. That you've been gone too long. That God's grace was for "back then," not "right now."

But here's the truth:

> *"Draw near to God, and He will draw near to you. Cleanse your hands, you sinners, and purify your hearts, you double-minded."*

> —*James 4:8*

There is no time limit on this invitation. The cross did not expire. The blood still flows.

You can come home today.

But What If I'm Not Ready?

Let's be honest — some of us *want* to come home, but feel stuck. We're still in the pigpen, still wrestling with guilt or confusion.

You don't have to *feel* ready. You just have to start moving.

In the parable, the father ran **while** the son was still "a long way off." He didn't wait for him to crawl the whole way back. He didn't lecture. He ran.

God moves the moment your heart turns.

But What If I Come Back and Fail Again?
You probably will.

But this isn't about being flawless. It's about being His.

God doesn't ask you to come back because you've conquered sin. He asks you to come back because He already has.

> *"Therefore, there is now no condemnation for those who are in Christ Jesus."*
>
> *—Romans 8:1*

The return isn't the end of the battle — it's the beginning of healing.

You come home not because you're perfect. You come home because He is.

Real Repentance, Real Return
Coming home doesn't mean pretending like nothing happened. It means owning it. Turning around. Coming back.

That's repentance — not just sorrow, but surrender.

> *"Return, Israel, to the LORD your God, for you have stumbled because of your guilt. Take words with you and return to the LORD. Say to Him, "Forgive all our guilt, and accept what is good, so that we may present the fruit of our lips."*
>
> *—Hosea 14:1–2*

God is not afraid of your stumble. He already saw it. He already made a way.

But He invites you to speak — to come with words, with humility, with honesty.

Not with bargains. Not with deals. Just a heart that says, *"I want to come home."*

What Coming Home Looks Like

For some, coming home will look like walking down an aisle. For others, it's kneeling by a bed. For some, it means baptism — a burial of the old self, a resurrection of the new. For others, it's rejoining a church family you've been running from.

But in every case, coming home means this:

You stop trying to outrun grace — and let it catch you.

You stop pretending you don't need God — and admit you do.

And then you collapse into His arms.

So What...

You've been gone. You've wandered. You've wondered if God's still listening, still waiting, still willing.

He is.

Not with a clipboard. Not with a cold stare. Not with "I told you so."

But with a robe. A ring. A feast.

All you have to do… is come.

And you can come home today.

14. Free at Last
Buried with Christ. Raised to Freedom

Nights on the interstate are loneliest after midnight. Mason could attest to that. He had driven almost six hours—past blinking truck-stop neon, past half-lit billboards promising cheap rooms and quick jackpots—because the silence inside his car was still kinder than the voices inside his head. Every song on the radio reminded him of what he had lost. Every mile marker felt like a sermon on regret.

Two months earlier he had stood in his kitchen and told his wife he'd "figure it out." Figure out his anger, his drinking, his double life. Figure out how to keep a Bible on the nightstand while hiding porn on a second phone. Figure out how to raise two children while bleeding out on the inside.

But he hadn't figured it out. And when his wife asked him to leave until he got help, the only destination that felt honest was the highway.

Somewhere after the state line, he prayed a sentence he barely believed:

> *"God, if You can still hear me,*
> *please say something."*

No bright light blinded him. No angel blocked the road. Yet the very act of speaking felt like a crack in the concrete—an opening neither shame nor cynicism could seal. It was the first honest prayer Mason had voiced in years, and it became the seed of everything that followed.

Tonight's chapter is for every Mason on the road—every soul who has reached the absolute end of self-help and discovered it is no help at all. The answer is not a better plan. The answer is a *new birth*.

1. The Question Behind Every Self-Help Failure

Self-help offers strategies—visualizations, mantras, micro-habits, grit. But none of those can answer the question that surfaces when the silence finally overpowers the noise:

> *"Can I ever be different at the core?"*

Scripture answers with a resounding yes—but not by tweaking the old self. By *burying* it and raising something completely new.

Paul defines the gospel this way:

> *"For I passed on to you as most important what I also received: that Christ died for our sins according to the Scriptures, that He was buried, that He was raised on the third day according to the Scriptures."*

> —*1 Corinthians 15:3-4*

The gospel is not advice; it is an accomplished event. Salvation is not a remodel of your moral habits; it is a resurrection of your dead spirit.

2. Why Good Intentions Cannot Save

The universal human dilemma is not low self-esteem or unmet potential. It is *sin*: active rebellion, passive indifference, and inherited corruption.

*"All missed the mark, and all fall short
of God's glorious standard."*

—Romans 3:23

Sin is treason against the holy King. No regimen of gratitude journals or ice baths can erase cosmic guilt. The penalty is death—first spiritual, finally physical, and ultimately eternal.

If the penalty is death, the remedy must address death. Enter the cross.

3. The Cross: Where Your Old Self Dies

Jesus did not add motivational fuel to humanity's engine; He took our sentence. On the cross He bore sin's full weight, satisfying justice and opening the floodgates of mercy. Yet the cross is not only substitution; it is participation.

*"We were buried with him through
immersion into death, so that just as
Christ was raised from the dead
through the glory of the Father, we too
can live a new life."*

—Romans 6:4

In God's design, the decisive moment where a sinner joins Christ's death and resurrection is **baptism**—the plunge of obedient faith, not a symbolic afterthought.

4. Faith That Obeys: The Response the Gospel Demands

After Peter's first gospel sermon, his hearers—cut to the heart—asked, "What shall we do?" (Acts 2:37). Peter did not prescribe journaling, volunteering, or passive belief.

He said:

> *"Repent and be immersed, each of*
> *you, in the name of Jesus Christ for the*
> *forgiveness of sins, and you will*
> *receive the gift of the Holy Spirit."*

—Acts 2:38

4.1 Believe
Saving faith is more than intellectual assent; it is trusting allegiance to the crucified and risen King. *(John 8 : 24)*

4.2 Repent
A Spirit-enabled about-face—hating the sin you once justified, surrendering the throne of your life to Christ. *(Luke 13 : 3)*

4.3 Confess
Open declaration that Jesus is Lord. Confession is the public seal of private belief. *(Romans 10:9-10)*

4.4 Be Baptized
Immersion unites the penitent believer with Christ's death, burial, and resurrection; washes away sins; clothes the believer with Christ; and grants the indwelling Spirit. *(Acts 22:16; Galatians 3:27; Colossians 2:12-13)*

Anything less stops short of the biblical pattern. Anything more adds human tradition to divine command.

5. What Really Happens in Baptism
1. **Sins are forgiven.** You emerge cleaner than Eden.

2. **You put on Christ.** Your old identity is replaced by His righteousness.

3. **You receive the Spirit.** The very life of God indwells you, empowering holiness from within.

4. **You enter Christ's body.** Salvation is personal but never private; baptism enrolls you in the family.

This is not magic water; it is God's chosen moment of union. The power is not in the ritual but in Jesus' blood meeting obedient faith.

6. Living the Freedom Baptism Begins

Freedom is not the absence of struggle; it is the presence of the Spirit who overcomes the flesh. You will still face temptation, but you now fight from victory, not for it.

"I say then, walk by the Spirit and you will certainly not carry out the desire of the flesh."

—Galatians 5:16

Grace becomes tutor (Titus 2:11-12), the Spirit becomes power (Romans 8:11), and the church becomes family (Ephesians 2:19).

7. Mason's Resurrection

Two weeks after that midnight prayer, Mason sat in a borrowed shirt and jeans beside a small baptistery. He confessed Jesus as Lord with a voice that trembled, not from doubt but from relief. When he rose from the water, his first words were, "It's done."

His marriage was not instantly healed. His addiction did not vanish overnight. But the man who drove six hours running from his failures died in that water. A new Mason began learning to walk—stumbling sometimes, standing often, always empowered by the same grace that saved him.

8. An Invitation No Book Can Replace

If you have reached the end of self-help—if you believe Jesus is the Christ, the Son of the living God—nothing stands between you and freedom except your response.

- **Do you believe?**
- **Will you repent?**
- **Will you confess Him?**
- **Will you be immersed into His death and resurrection?**

You can do that today. Wherever you are, find a Christian who teaches and practices the New Testament pattern and say, *"I want to be buried and raised with Christ."* If you need help, reach out—this book's final pages include resources and contacts of churches committed to biblical teaching.

9. So What...

Self-help could never free you. Religion could only enslave you differently. But Jesus—the crucified, risen, reigning King—offers **true freedom**:

> *"So if the Son sets you free,*
> *you really will be free."*
>
> —*John 8:36*

Today, lay down every strategy, every shame, every sin. Die with Him. Rise with Him. Walk with Him.

Free at last. Not because you tried harder, but because grace finished what your grit never could.

Appendix: Now What?
Walking Fully in Your New Freedom

Core Scriptures for Further Study

Spend unhurried time with each passage. These verses anchor your understanding of salvation, grace, and life in Christ.

A New Heart *Ezekiel 36:25–27* God promises transformation, not self-repair.

Gospel Summary *1 Corinthians 15:1–4* The death, burial, and resurrection of Jesus—our foundation.

Salvation Moment *Acts 2:36–41* The first gospel sermon and response: *repent and be baptized.*

New Life *Romans 6:1–7* Baptism is where the old self dies and a new life begins.

Clothed with Christ *Galatians 3:26–27* You become part of Christ and His family in baptism.

Spirit-Led Freedom *Romans 8:1–11* Life in the Spirit replaces life in the flesh.

Grace Trains *Titus 2:11–14* Grace not only saves—it teaches and transforms.

***

A Clear Response Pattern (Based on Scripture)

If you're wondering how to obey the gospel, here's what Scripture shows time and time again:

1. *Believe the Gospel*

Faith is more than agreement—it's personal trust in Jesus as Savior and King. (John 8:24; Hebrews 11:6)

2. *Repent of Sin*

Repentance is a change of heart and direction, turning from sin and turning to God. (Luke 13:3; Acts 17:30)

3. *Confess Christ*

Speak your faith out loud: "Jesus is Lord." This confession anchors your new identity. (Romans 10:9–10; Matthew 10:32)

4. *Be Baptized into Christ*

Be buried and raised with Him through baptism. In that moment, your sins are washed away, and you receive the gift of the Holy Spirit. (Acts 2:38; Romans 6:3–4; Galatians 3:27; Acts 22:16)

***

What Happens in Baptism

- Your **sins are forgiven** (Acts 2:38)
- You are **united with Christ's death and resurrection** (Romans 6:4)
- You **clothe yourself with Christ** (Galatians 3:27)
- You receive the **Holy Spirit** (Acts 2:38)
- You are added to **Christ's body, the church** (1 Corinthians 12:13)

This isn't just symbolic. It's the moment where saving faith becomes obedient faith. You die with Christ, and you rise with Him—*free at last.*

***

After Baptism: Your New Priorities
Your new life doesn't end at baptism—it begins. Here's how to grow:

1. *The Word*
Start with the Gospel of John and the book of Acts. Read slowly. Mark verses. Ask questions. Let God speak.

2. *Prayer*
Talk to God every day—honestly, quietly, openly. Schedule time. Build the habit.

3. *Community*
Find a local church that teaches the truth of the New Testament. Worship weekly. Grow with others. If you need helping finding a place, contact the author. If there is not a place, we can assist you in setting up a community in your home.

4. *Accountability*
Don't isolate. Share your journey with other believers. Confess your struggles. Celebrate progress.

5. *Service*
Ask, "Where can I help?" God saved you *for* good works. Start small. Stay faithful.

***

Need Help Taking the Next Step?

If you're ready to obey the gospel—or want to study further—we would love to hear from you. Whether you're unsure about baptism, need prayer, or want someone to walk with you, reach out.

Contact:
Marty Hale
Lubbock, Texas
marty@straighttruthpress.com

You don't have to do this alone. You were never meant to.